AI in Mind Mapping

REVOLUTIONIZING THOUGHT ORGANIZATION

Dr. Salwa Elmeawad

ELDONUSA Publishing

Contents

1

ABOUT THE AUTHOR

AI
in Mind Mapping
Revolutionizing Thought Organization
By
Dr. Salwa Elmeawad

Dr. Salwa Elmeawad stands out as a luminary in both the academic and community service spheres. With an illustrious career at the helm of adult services manager at Queens Library, she has profoundly impacted the field of information access and literacy. Dr. Elmeawad's educational journey is marked by not one, but two doctoral degrees,

1

showcasing her dedication to lifelong learning and expertise in both organizational leadership and information systems and technology.

Her commitment extends beyond the academic realm into spirited community service. As the Distinguished Lieutenant Governor for the Kiwanis Queens East Division, Dr. Elmeawad plays a pivotal role in steering community-focused initiatives and fostering a spirit of service. Her role as a board member of the KPTC further exemplifies her dedication to impactful community work, particularly in areas of pediatric care and trauma prevention.

Dr. Elmeawad's passion for mentorship and youth development is evident through her involvement with the Benjamin Cardozo High School Key Club. As a lead mentor, coach, and advisor, she guides young minds in their personal and professional development, instilling in them the values of leadership and community service.

Her multifaceted expertise and unwavering commitment to both academic excellence and community service make Dr. Salwa Elmeawad a distinguished figure in her field and an inspiration to many.

2

PREFACE

Welcome to "AI in Mind Mapping: Revolutionizing Thought Organization," a comprehensive exploration of the synergy between artificial intelligence (AI) and mind mapping. This book is designed to bridge the gap between the rich, intuitive process of mind mapping and the powerful, analytical capabilities of AI. It serves as both a guide and an inspiration for harnessing these tools to enhance cognitive abilities, boost creativity, and improve decision-making processes.

Purpose

The primary purpose of this book is to demystify the integration of AI with traditional mind mapping techniques, providing readers with a clear understanding of how this convergence can be applied to real-world challenges. By blending theoretical knowledge with practical applications, the book aims to showcase how AI can automate, enhance, and expand the possibilities of mind mapping, making it a more powerful tool for organizing thoughts, brainstorming ideas, and managing complex information.

Significance

In our increasingly data-driven world, the ability to quickly synthesize information and generate new ideas is invaluable. AI in mind mapping represents a frontier in cognitive technology, where the human capacity for creativity meets the machine's ability for rapid data processing and pattern recognition. This book underscores the significance of this integration, illustrating how it can lead to more dynamic and effective thinking and planning methods. Moreover, it addresses the growing need for tools that can enhance cognitive productivity in various domains, from education to business to personal development.

Structure of the Book

The book is organized into detailed chapters that begin with foundational concepts of mind mapping and AI, gradually moving towards more complex applications and futuristic insights. Each chapter includes real-world examples, case studies, and practical advice to ensure that the concepts are accessible and applicable. Additionally, the book offers a comprehensive review of the latest tools and technologies in AI-powered mind mapping, providing readers with the resources to begin their journey in revolutionizing their thought processes.

As we embark on this exciting exploration of AI in mind mapping, our hope is that you, the reader, will find valuable insights and practical tools to transform your approach to organizing and generating ideas. This journey promises not only to enhance your cognitive abilities but also to open up new pathways for innovation and creativity in your personal and professional life.

Welcome aboard, and let's start mapping the future together.

Dr. Salwa Elmeawad

3

WHO SHOULD READ THIS BOOK?

"AI in Mind Mapping: Revolutionizing Thought Organization" is meticulously designed to cater to a wide range of readers, from professionals seeking to enhance their strategic thinking and problem-solving skills, to students aiming to boost their academic performance through more effective study techniques. Here are the specific groups that will find this book particularly beneficial:

Professionals

Professionals across various industries will find this book invaluable for learning how to integrate AI with mind mapping to optimize decision-making, enhance problem-solving skills, and boost productivity. Whether you're in business, healthcare, IT, or any field where strategic planning and clear thinking are paramount, this book offers tools to streamline processes and foster innovation.

Educators and Trainers

Educators and trainers can utilize the insights and techniques discussed to enhance their teaching strategies and curriculum designs. This book provides methodologies for using AI-powered mind mapping as a pedagogical tool to promote engagement, enhance learning outcomes, and facilitate a deeper understanding of complex subjects.

Students

Students at any level of education will benefit from understanding how AI can augment traditional mind mapping techniques to improve note-taking, studying, and project management. The book outlines strategies to enhance learning efficiency and academic performance, making it a valuable resource for high school, college, and graduate students.

Project Managers and Team Leaders

Project managers and team leaders looking to improve collaboration, project planning, and execution will find the book's focus on AI-enhanced mind mapping tools particularly useful. It offers strategies to facilitate better brainstorming sessions, organize information more effectively, and manage projects with greater precision.

Researchers

Researchers who deal with large volumes of information and require effective ways to organize, analyze, and generate insights will appreciate the book's emphasis on advanced AI techniques in mind mapping. It provides methodologies for synthesizing data and accelerating the research process through innovative thinking frameworks.

Tech Enthusiasts

Tech enthusiasts and early adopters interested in the latest advancements in AI and cognitive technologies will find this book an exciting read. It not only covers current applications but also speculates on future developments in the integration of AI with cognitive tools like mind mapping.

Personal Development Seekers

Individuals interested in personal growth and improved mental organization can leverage the techniques discussed to better manage their daily tasks, set clearer goals, and enhance their creativity. This book provides practical advice on using AI-enhanced mind mapping for personal development planning and problem-solving.

Business Strategists and Entrepreneurs

Business strategists, entrepreneurs, and innovators looking for new ways to structure their thinking and explore creative solutions will benefit from the strategic insights into AI-driven mind mapping. The book offers guidance on leveraging these tools to stay ahead in competitive markets by fostering innovative thinking and efficient strategy formulation.

Happy Reading!

Dr. Salwa Elmeawad

4

WHY THIS BOOK IS ESSENTIAL READING?

In today's fast-paced and increasingly complex world, the ability to quickly organize thoughts, generate creative solutions, and make informed decisions is more crucial than ever. "AI in Mind Mapping: Revolutionizing Thought Organization" is essential reading for several compelling reasons, addressing both the need for advanced cognitive tools and the integration of cutting-edge technology in everyday processes.

Harnessing the Power of AI

Artificial Intelligence is transforming every sector of society, from healthcare to finance to education. This book provides a thorough understanding of how AI can be applied to the process of mind mapping, which has traditionally been a manual, time-consuming task. By automating aspects of mind mapping, AI enables users to process information faster, identify relationships between concepts more efficiently, and generate more comprehensive maps with less effort. This book explains these processes in a clear and accessible way, making it an essential guide for anyone looking to leverage AI in practical and effective ways.

Enhancing Cognitive Abilities

Mind mapping is a powerful technique for visualizing information, improving memory, and enhancing creativity. By incorporating AI, these benefits are magnified. AI algorithms can suggest connections and ideas that may not be immediately obvious, helping to deepen understanding and foster innovative thinking. This book provides practical strategies and examples of how AI-enhanced mind mapping can be used to solve complex problems, make better decisions, and brainstorm more effectively.

Improving Productivity and Efficiency

For professionals and organizations, efficiency is often a key determinant of success. This book demonstrates how integrating AI with mind mapping can streamline workflows and enhance productivity. By automating data organization and pattern recognition, AI-enhanced mind maps reduce the cognitive load on users, freeing them to focus on higher-level strategic thinking and creativity. This is particularly beneficial in project management, strategic planning, and any area where clear, quick decision-making is required.

Future-Proofing Skills

As AI continues to evolve, understanding how to interact with and leverage this technology becomes increasingly important. This book not only educates readers on current applications but also prepares them for future developments in AI technology. By mastering AI-enhanced mind mapping now, readers can stay ahead of the curve in their respective fields, maintaining a competitive edge and adapting to future changes in technology more easily.

Broad Applicability

Whether you are a student looking to improve your study techniques, a professional keen on enhancing your productivity, or a leader tasked with driving innovation in your organization, the strategies discussed in this book are applicable across a broad range of contexts and challenges. The book's diverse audience—ranging from educators to business executives—underscores its relevance to a wide spectrum of readers who can benefit from AI's potential to transform traditional mind mapping into a dynamic and powerful tool.

Engaging Content

Beyond its practical applications, this book is designed to be engaging and accessible. It demystifies complex topics and provides real-world examples and case studies that illustrate the powerful combination of AI and mind mapping. This approach ensures that readers not only understand the theoretical aspects but also see how they can be applied in practical, everyday scenarios.

5

Chapter 1: Understanding Mind Mapping

Mind mapping is a versatile and powerful tool that has transformed how individuals and organizations visualize information, brainstorm ideas, and manage projects. This section of the book aims to delve deep into the essence of mind mapping, explaining its core principles, benefits, and applications. It lays the groundwork for later discussions on enhancing these techniques with artificial intelligence.

What is Mind Mapping?

Mind mapping is a graphical technique used to represent ideas, tasks, or other items linked to and arranged around a central concept. By visually organizing information, mind mapping helps users to comprehend, recall, and generate new ideas more effectively. It typically involves creating a diagram that branches out from a central keyword or idea, with related tasks, ideas, or notes radiating outward.

Historical Background

The concept of mind mapping has been traced back to the third century but was popularized in the late 20th century by British psychologist Tony Buzan. He argued that traditional notes, with their linear and sequential format, restrict the brain's potential to make connections and generate new ideas. Mind mapping, by contrast, mirrors the brain's associative thought processes, making it more natural and effective.

Core Principles of Mind Mapping

1. **Central Image:** A mind map is typically organized around a single, central concept that is usually depicted as an image in the center of the map. This helps to anchor the map and focus attention.

2. **Associative Branching:** From the central image, major themes radiate outward in the form of branches, which then subdivide into smaller branches. This hierarchical and associative approach facilitates understanding and memory recall.

3. **Keywords:** Each branch carries a keyword or short phrase that summarizes an idea or concept, reducing the cognitive load and making the information easy to navigate.

4. **Visual Triggers:** Mind maps use colors, images, and symbols to enhance memory and differentiation between branches, making the map more engaging and easier to recall.

5. **Non-linear Layout:** The spatial arrangement allows users to jump between ideas freely, encouraging a more creative exploration of relationships.

Benefits of Mind Mapping
Mind mapping offers several cognitive and practical benefits:

- **Enhances Memory and Recall:** The use of images, colors, and spatial organization in mind maps helps in better retention and recall of information.
- **Boosts Creativity:** The non-linear layout encourages a free flow of ideas, making it an excellent tool for brainstorming sessions.
- **Simplifies Complex Information:** Mind maps can break down complex topics into simpler, more digestible components.

- **Improves Organization and Planning:** The visual overview provided by a mind map helps in better organizing thoughts and planning projects or events.
- **Facilitates Collaboration:** Mind maps can be used as a shared knowledge base, enhancing collaboration among team members.

Applications Across Fields

Mind mapping is utilized in various fields and for diverse purposes:

- **Education:** For note-taking, summarizing information, and preparing for exams.
- **Business:** For strategic planning, meeting management, and enhancing presentations.
- **Personal Development:** For goal setting, personal reflection, or planning life events.
- **Project Management:** For task breakdown, resource allocation, and timeline planning.

The Concept and Historical Evolution:

Mind mapping is a dynamic tool that facilitates the visual organization of information, making complex ideas simpler and more accessible. This section delves into the concept of mind mapping, tracing its roots and evolution over time to provide a comprehensive understanding of this powerful cognitive tool.

The Concept of Mind Mapping:

Mind mapping is a method used to visually organize information around a central concept or idea. It involves creating a diagram that branches out to illustrate the relationships between a central theme and associated topics. Each branch of a mind map contains a key word or image that represents an idea or task, which can further branch out into subtopics. This method leverages the natural inclination of the human brain towards making associative connections, rather than linear note-taking.

Definition and Structure

A mind map is a diagram used to visually organize information. It is structured around a single, central concept, from which related ideas and facts radiate. These ideas are laid out in a branching structure, resembling a tree with numerous branches. Each branch represents a key aspect or theme of the central concept, and these branches can further subdivide into smaller branches, which detail more specific ideas or data points.

The typical components of a mind map include:

- **Central Node:** This is the core idea or theme from which all other parts of the mind map extend. It is usually represented visually by an image or a word placed at the center of the map.
- **Main Branches:** These are thick lines or arrows that connect the central node to major subtopics or themes, demonstrating the primary associative connections.
- **Sub-branches:** Stemming from each main branch, these thinner lines or arrows represent more detailed thoughts or information pertaining to each subtopic.
- **Keywords and Images:** Each branch and sub-branch typically contains a single keyword or image that encapsulates the essence of the idea, making the map both concise and memory-friendly.

Purpose and Utility

The primary purpose of a mind map is to facilitate easier learning and recall through visual stimulation and the arrangement of information in a naturally intuitive format. Mind maps exploit the brain's propensity for image processing and color recognition, elements that enhance memory and learning. They are particularly effective for:

- **Brainstorming:** Generating new ideas and freely exploring creative solutions.
- **Note-taking:** Organizing information gleaned from meetings, lectures, or readings in a way that's easy to review and understand.
- **Studying and Memorization:** Structuring educational content in a visually engaging manner that aligns with natural memory pathways.
- **Project and Task Management:** Visualizing tasks, deadlines, and dependencies in project planning or personal productivity.

Cognitive Foundations

Mind mapping aligns with several cognitive theories and psychological observations:

- **Associative Learning:** The brain naturally works by making associations rather than thinking linearly. Mind maps mimic this associative pattern, which is why they can improve creativity and problem-solving skills.
- **Dual Coding Theory:** This theory suggests that information is easier to recall when it is stored in both verbal and visual forms. Mind maps combine short, punchy text (keywords) with visual elements like colors and images, which facilitates better memory retention.
- **Gestalt Principles:** These principles state that the human mind seeks to perceive a unified whole in complex arrangements of information. Mind maps organize discrete pieces of information into related clusters that are perceived together, making complex ideas more digestible.

The concept of mind mapping leverages the brain's inherent capabilities for visual processing, association, and gestalt organization. By understanding the fundamental structure and purpose of mind mapping, users can effectively apply this tool across various domains to enhance their cognitive processes, from creative endeavors and learning to systematic planning and information management. This visualization strategy not only simplifies the absorption of complex information but also significantly improves the ability to recall and apply knowledge effectively.

Origins of the Concept:

The use of graphical techniques to map out information is not a modern invention. Historical examples include the Porphyrian tree, a diagram used in the Middle Ages to categorize Aristotle's categories of understanding, and the works of Ramon Llull in the 13th century, who created complex systems of diagrams to help explain his philosophical ideas.

However, the term "mind map" and the specific techniques associated with modern mind mapping were developed and popularized by British psychologist Tony Buzan in the 1970s. Buzan introduced mind mapping as a way to utilize the full range of cortical skills—word, image, number, logic, rhythm, color, and spatial awareness—to unlock the potential of the brain. He argued that traditional note-taking methods were linear and restrictive, whereas the brain works in a much more spontaneous and organized manner.

Ancient and Medieval Precursors

The use of graphical representations to organize knowledge and enhance memory has been documented throughout history. In the third century, Porphyry of Tyros created the "Porphyrian Tree," a diagram used to classify and organize Aristotle's categories, effectively laying the groundwork for later visual thinking tools. During the medieval period, philosophers and theologians used intricate diagrams known as "memory palaces" and other mnemonic devices to visualize complex theological and philosophical arguments.

Renaissance Developments

The Renaissance brought a renewed interest in knowledge visualization, influenced by an upsurge in scientific inquiry and exploration. Figures like Ramon Llull and later Giordano Bruno developed sophisticated mnemonic systems that used diagrams to represent knowledge visually. These early forms of knowledge mapping were crucial in helping scholars and thinkers of the period manage the increasing influx of information brought about by the printing press and expanding scientific discoveries.

20th Century Formalization

The formal concept of mind mapping as we know it today began to take shape in the 20th century, particularly with the work of British psychologist Tony Buzan in the 1970s. Buzan coined the term "mind map" and introduced the technique as a revolutionary tool for learning and thinking. He argued that traditional notes, with their linear and sequential format, did not match the way the brain actually processes and retrieves information, which is much more dynamic and associative.

Buzan's method was designed to utilize this natural cognitive architecture, encouraging users to start with a central idea and radiate outward in all directions, forming a branching tree of related concepts. This was a significant shift from previous models, emphasizing creativity, color, and the use of images and symbols—all elements that engage the brain's capacities more fully than linear text alone.

The Role of Educational Theorists

Parallel to Buzan's contributions, educational theorists and cognitive psychologists were exploring similar ideas about learning and information retention. These scholars focused on how non-linear and graphic organizers could enhance learning by tapping into the brain's inherent capabilities for spatial and visual processing. Their research supported and expanded the theoretical foundations of mind mapping, helping to integrate it more fully into educational methodologies.

Digital Evolution

The advent of digital technology has greatly expanded the accessibility and functionality of mind mapping. Software tools now offer powerful features such as real-time collaboration, integration with other digital platforms, and capabilities for including multimedia content. This digital evolution has transformed mind mapping from a primarily individual and analog practice into a versatile tool used globally in education, business, and personal productivity.

The origins of mind mapping stretch from ancient visual techniques developed for memory and knowledge organization to its formalization in the 20th century and expansion in the digital age. Understanding these roots not only enriches our appreciation of mind mapping but also underscores its enduring value as a tool for learning and creative thinking. This historical perspective highlights how mind mapping has continuously evolved to meet the needs of its users, adapting to new intellectual and technological landscapes.

Historical Evolution

Mind mapping gained prominence as a popular cognitive tool following its formal introduction by Tony Buzan on the BBC TV series "Use Your Head" in the late 1970s. In his series and subsequent books, Buzan laid out the theory behind mind mapping and its advantages for learning and memory, which helped spread its use in educational and business settings.

Over the decades, mind mapping has evolved from being a paper-based technique to a digital one, thanks to the advent of personal computing and the internet. Modern software tools allow for the creation of digital mind maps that can be edited and shared instantly with others across the globe. These tools often incorporate features such as real-time collaboration, multimedia integration, and cloud storage, enhancing the functionality and applicability of mind maps in various contexts.

Early Intellectual Tools

The history of organizing knowledge visually begins well before the term "mind map" was coined. Ancient philosophers like Porphyry of Tyros employed tree-like diagrams to categorize Aristotle's categories of understanding, creating what is now known as the "Porphyrian Tree." These early diagrams were mnemonic devices, designed to help users remember information through spatial and associative qualities. During the medieval period, similar methods were widely used by scholars to organize complex theological and philosophical data, often depicted in illuminated manuscripts.

Renaissance to Enlightenment

During the Renaissance, thinkers such as Ramon Llull and later Giordano Bruno developed complex mnemonic systems and wheels of knowledge that used visual symbols and arrangements to facilitate the storage and retrieval of information. These were not mind maps in the modern sense but shared the underlying principle of using spatial and associative relationships to manage knowledge. The Enlightenment continued this tradition with figures like Gottfried Wilhelm Leibniz, who experimented with graphic encyclopedic systems to represent all human knowledge.

20th Century: The Buzan Era

The contemporary concept of mind mapping was introduced by British psychologist Tony Buzan in the 1970s. Inspired by both the need for efficient information management in the modern educational system and by his own research into brain function and memory, Buzan formalized mind mapping as a technique with specific rules and practices. He promoted mind mapping as a tool that mirrors the way the brain processes information — associatively and non-linearly — as opposed to traditional note-taking methods.

Buzan's work led to the widespread adoption of mind mapping in educational settings, where it was used to help students organize notes, plan essays, and prepare for exams. His books and television appearances popularized the concept globally, making it a standard tool in the fields of education, business, and personal productivity.

Digital Revolution

The introduction of personal computers and the internet marked a significant turning point in the evolution of mind mapping. Digital mind mapping tools began to appear in the late 20th and early 21st centuries, transforming the practice from a manual, paper-based exercise into a dynamic and interactive digital experience. These tools offered new features, such as the ability to include hyperlinks, documents, and multimedia, and enabled real-time collaboration across different locations.

Digital mind mapping software has made the creation and sharing of mind maps faster and more efficient, allowing for more complex and data-rich maps. Additionally, the integration of mind mapping software with other digital productivity tools has further expanded its applications and utility in various professional fields.

The historical evolution of mind mapping from ancient mnemonic devices to sophisticated digital tools reflects its fundamental role in enhancing human cognitive capabilities. Each phase in its development has adapted the basic principles of visual organization to the needs and technologies of the era, confirming mind mapping's versatility and effectiveness. Understanding this historical context enriches our appreciation of mind mapping and underscores its potential as a universal tool for learning, creativity, and organization in the information age.

The Digital Transformation

The transition to digital mind mapping has significantly expanded the scope and utility of the tool. Digital mind maps can handle large amounts of data, integrate with other digital tools, and include various types of media (texts, images, links, videos), making them more versatile and powerful than their paper-based counterparts. This evolution has made mind mapping more accessible and applicable in diverse fields including project management, software development, education, and business planning.

Understanding the concept and historical evolution of mind mapping is essential for appreciating its value and versatility. From ancient philosophical diagrams to modern digital tools, mind mapping has continuously evolved to meet the changing needs of its users. It remains a vital technique for organizing thoughts, enhancing memory, and fostering creative thinking, proving its enduring relevance in a world that increasingly values visual and nonlinear thinking.

Emergence of Digital Mind Mapping

The digital transformation of mind mapping began in the late 20th century as personal computers became more prevalent and software capabilities expanded. Early digital mind mapping tools were simple, offering basic functionalities that replicated the process of drawing a mind map on paper but on a computer screen. These initial versions already provided significant advantages over paper, including easy editing, cleaner presentation, and the ability to store and retrieve maps electronically.

Advancements in Software

As technology progressed, so did the features available in mind mapping software. Modern mind mapping tools now offer a range of sophisticated functionalities:

- **Hyperlinking and Attachments:** Users can embed hyperlinks, documents, videos, and other multimedia directly into their mind maps, turning them into comprehensive knowledge management systems.
- **Collaboration Features:** Many tools support real-time collaboration, allowing multiple users to work on the same mind map simultaneously, regardless of their physical location. This has made mind mapping an invaluable tool for remote teams and online education.
- **Integration Capabilities:** Today's mind mapping software often integrates seamlessly with other productivity tools, such as project management software, calendar apps, and data analysis tools. This integration facilitates a more holistic approach to information management and project planning.
- **Customization and Scalability:** Digital tools allow for extensive customization of the mind mapping process, including templates, style options, and automated layouts. Maps can also be scaled more easily, handling complex information that would be unwieldy on paper.

Impact on Usage and Popularity

The digital transformation has significantly broadened the user base of mind mapping. With the advent of mobile computing, mind mapping apps have become available on smartphones and tablets, making the tool accessible anytime and anywhere. This mobility has increased the use of mind maps in everyday tasks such as personal organization, quick note-taking, and on-the-go brainstorming.

Educational and Business Transformation

In educational contexts, digital mind maps have become a tool for interactive learning, enabling students to engage directly with the material by creating and manipulating their own maps. Teachers can incorporate mind maps into their teaching materials, enhancing the visual learning experience and catering to different learning styles.

In the business world, the ability to share and collaborate on mind maps easily has streamlined project management and strategic planning. Teams can visualize project timelines, brainstorm ideas, and outline business strategies in a dynamic, interactive format that can be updated in real time as projects evolve.

Future Prospects

Looking ahead, the digital transformation of mind mapping is poised to integrate more deeply with emerging technologies such as AI and big data analytics. AI, for instance, could offer predictive insights, automatic clustering of information, or even suggest connections based on data trends, enhancing the mind mapping process beyond human limitations. As technology continues to evolve, so too will the capabilities and applications of digital mind mapping, potentially transforming it into an even more powerful cognitive and organizational tool.

The digital transformation of mind mapping has not only preserved its core principles but has expanded its utility and effectiveness manifold. By transitioning from paper to pixels, mind mapping has adapted to the digital age, offering users unprecedented flexibility and power in organizing and visualizing information. This evolution underscores the adaptability of mind mapping to meet the changing needs of its users, ensuring its relevance in a digital future.

Core Principles and Cognitive Benefits:

Mind mapping is a visual organization tool that is not only intuitive but also deeply aligned with the natural operations of human cognition. To fully appreciate its usefulness, it is essential to understand the core principles that underpin mind mapping and the cognitive benefits that it offers.

Core Principles of Mind Mapping

The effectiveness of mind mapping stems from several core principles that guide its design and use:

Centralization:

At the heart of every mind map is a central theme or idea. This central concept anchors all other information, helping to contextualize and relate the incoming ideas to a core understanding, which aids in cognitive processing and recall.

The Role of Centralization in Mind Mapping

Centralization is not merely a structural feature; it is essential for organizing and processing information effectively. By placing a central idea or theme at the center of a mind map, users create a focal point that guides the development of related ideas and ensures that all subsequent thoughts and information connect back to this central theme. This approach mirrors how our brain naturally organizes information, with a central concept and associated details branching out like neurons.

How Centralization Enhances Mind Mapping

Focus and Clarity: The central idea in a mind map clarifies the purpose of the mapping exercise. It provides a clear focus, helping users stay on track and avoid deviating into unrelated areas. This focus is crucial for effective brainstorming and problem-solving, as it ensures that all generated ideas are relevant to the central theme.

Contextual Framework: Centralization offers a contextual backbone for all the information on the map. It helps users understand how various pieces of information are interrelated and how they all tie back to the main theme. This context is vital for comprehensive learning and understanding, as it allows for a holistic view of the subject matter.

Encourages Association: By starting with a central idea, the mind is encouraged to think associatively, exploring different facets of the main theme through branching paths. This associative thinking is a natural strength of the human brain and is particularly effective for generating creative solutions and making complex connections.

Aids Memory Retention: Centralization helps in anchoring the information in memory. The central concept becomes a strong retrieval cue, making it easier to recall the surrounding information that branches out from this central point. This is particularly useful in educational settings, where students can use the central idea to recall details during exams or discussions.

Simplifies Complexity: For complex topics, centralization simplifies the structure of information, making it easier to digest. By breaking down a broad theme into sub-themes that radiate from a central point, mind maps allow users to approach complex information step-by-step, reducing cognitive overload and enhancing understanding.

Centralization is a core principle of mind mapping that has profound implications for cognitive processing. It not only provides focus, clarity, and context but also facilitates associative thinking and simplifies complex information. This principle ensures that mind maps are effective tools for learning, brainstorming, and organizing information, making them invaluable in both educational and professional contexts. By understanding and effectively utilizing the principle of centralization, users can maximize the cognitive benefits of mind mapping, leading to improved memory, creativity, and problem-solving abilities.

Radiant Structure:

From the central idea, branches radiate outward to represent major sub-themes or categories. These branches further subdivide into finer details, mimicking the way that thoughts expand and connect in the human mind. This structure encourages a hierarchical yet interconnected approach to information organization.

The Role of Radiant Structure in Mind Mapping

In a mind map, the central concept is visually connected to major subtopics or ideas through branches, which in turn may branch out into more specific details. This branching continues as needed to represent the complexity and richness of the information related to the central idea. The radiant structure promotes a free-form but organized approach to brainstorming and information sorting, which is both flexible and systematic.

How Radiant Structure Enhances Mind Mapping

Natural Cognitive Flow: The radiant structure of a mind map closely resembles the way the human brain works. Like neurons that branch out in the brain, each idea in a mind map can spark new associations, leading to a rich web of connected thoughts. This layout leverages the brain's capacity for pattern recognition and association, which enhances cognitive processing and creativity.

Visual Simplicity and Clarity: By spreading out ideas radially, mind maps avoid the clutter and linear constraints of traditional note-taking. This clear separation of ideas and branches makes it easier to locate and navigate through different sections of information, improving comprehension and recall.

Enhanced Memory Retention: The spatial arrangement in mind maps helps in encoding the information more effectively into memory. Visual and spatial cues are powerful memory aids, and the radiant structure of mind maps utilizes these to enhance learning and recall. This is especially useful in educational and learning contexts where recalling vast amounts of information accurately is crucial.

Encourages Comprehensive Exploration: The non-linear nature of mind maps encourages a holistic view of topics. As new ideas are generated, they can be added anywhere on the map without disrupting the existing structure. This flexibility is conducive to exploring complex subjects comprehensively, as it allows the mapper to jump between and link different ideas freely.

Facilitates Problem Solving: The radiant structure allows for a visual representation of problems and their possible solutions, showing how different variables and factors connect and impact each other. This can be incredibly useful for diagnosing issues, brainstorming solutions, and visualizing the paths of influence or consequence within a given problem space.

The radiant structure is a core principle of mind mapping that significantly contributes to its effectiveness as a cognitive tool. This layout not only enhances the visual appeal and clarity of the map but also aligns with natural brain functions such as associative thinking and spatial recognition. By organizing information radially around a central theme, mind maps facilitate a deeper understanding, better memory retention, and more dynamic problem-solving capabilities. Whether used for learning, brainstorming, or planning, the radiant structure of mind maps offers a powerful way to visualize and manage complex information.

Use of Keywords:

Each branch is ideally labeled with a single keyword or a short phrase that captures the essence of the information. This practice supports cognitive efficiency by reducing complex information to its most essential form, making it easier to remember and mentally manipulate.

Importance of Keywords in Mind Mapping

In mind mapping, each branch typically carries a keyword or a very short phrase that summarizes the concept or idea it represents. This focused approach to labeling branches is crucial because it helps to maintain the clarity and efficiency of the map. Keywords act as mental hooks that quickly lead the user back to a more detailed network of thoughts and associations.

Benefits of Using Keywords in Mind Mapping

Cognitive Efficiency: Keywords streamline cognitive processing by reducing the complexity of information. When a mind map uses succinct keywords, it requires less mental effort to absorb and recall the information. This efficiency is particularly beneficial in scenarios like studying, brainstorming, or presenting complex ideas.

Enhanced Memory Retention: The use of keywords helps in encoding information into long-term memory more effectively. Keywords function as cues or triggers that can evoke a larger body of information when recalled. This mnemonic principle is essential in educational contexts where recall of vast amounts of data is required.

Quick Reference and Navigation: Keywords allow users to quickly navigate through a mind map without getting bogged down by too much detail at once. They make it easy to skim the map for information, making mind maps particularly useful for review sessions or during presentations where time is limited.

Stimulates Associative Thinking: Keywords encourage the brain to make connections not only within the context of the mind map but also with other external knowledge and ideas. This associative capability is crucial for creativity and problem-solving, where linking disparate ideas can lead to innovative solutions.

Focuses Discussion and Thought: By limiting each branch to a keyword or a simple phrase, the mind map remains focused and uncluttered. This clarity helps users stay on topic during discussions and thought processes, reducing the likelihood of diversion and enhancing the productivity of cognitive efforts.

Implementing Keywords Effectively in Mind Maps

To maximize the benefits of using keywords in mind maps, consider the following tips:

- **Choose Precisely:** Select words that are evocative and rich in meaning. A good keyword can encapsulate an entire idea or concept, which aids in deeper understanding and recall.
- **Be Consistent:** Use a consistent method for selecting keywords to maintain uniformity across the map, which helps in easier navigation and interpretation.
- **Integrate Imagery:** Whenever possible, accompany keywords with images or symbols. Visual cues reinforce the connection

between the keyword and the concept it represents, enhancing memory and understanding.

- **Limit One Keyword per Branch:** Stick to one keyword per branch to maintain simplicity and focus. This discipline in keyword usage ensures that the mind map doesn't become overcrowded or confusing.

The use of keywords is a fundamental principle in mind mapping that significantly enhances its cognitive benefits. By carefully selecting and implementing keywords, mind mappers can create powerful tools for learning, memory, and creative problem-solving. This strategic use of succinct labels ensures that mind maps remain effective as visual and cognitive aids, helping users to organize their thoughts efficiently and clearly.

Visual-Spatial Arrangement:

Mind maps leverage spatial orientation to help structure information, enabling users to see the relationships between different parts of the map clearly. This visual arrangement exploits the brain's innate ability to recognize and recall visual patterns.

The Role of Visual-Spatial Arrangement in Mind Mapping

Mind maps are distinctively organized in a radial, non-linear format that spreads from a central node. This spatial organization not only helps in distinguishing different ideas and their sub-categories but also visually represents the relationships between these concepts. The arrangement takes advantage of the brain's predisposition towards processing visual information faster than text, using space effectively to enhance understanding and memory.

Benefits of Visual-Spatial Arrangement in Mind Mapping

Enhanced Cognitive Clarity: The spatial distribution of information in a mind map helps minimize cognitive overload. Each branch and its subsequent sub-branches are arranged to reduce clutter, making each element distinct and easier to focus on. This clarity is crucial in helping users understand complex information structures and retrieve data from memory efficiently.

Improves Information Recall: Spatial relationships established in a mind map can serve as powerful mnemonic aids. The brain can often remember information better when it is associated with a specific location within a visual field. This spatial memory is particularly effective when revisiting a mind map for review, as the position of the information can trigger recall of the content.

Facilitates Pattern Recognition: By visually organizing data, mind maps enable users to see patterns and relationships that might not be as obvious in linear text. This capability is essential for synthesizing information, spotting trends, and understanding complex systems at a glance.

Encourages Holistic Viewing: The radial structure of a mind map encourages users to view information holistically rather than sequentially. This comprehensive view supports integrative thinking, where connections across different areas of knowledge can be made, fostering creative solutions and comprehensive problem-solving strategies.

Aids in Quick Navigation and Accessibility: A well-organized mind map allows users to navigate large amounts of information quickly. The visual-spatial arrangement makes it easy to zoom in on details or zoom out for an overview, making mind maps exceptionally adaptable to various tasks, from detailed analysis to broad strategic planning.

Implementing Visual-Spatial Arrangement Effectively

To optimize the cognitive benefits of visual-spatial arrangement in mind maps, consider the following best practices:

- **Balance Simplicity and Detail:** Ensure that each branch is spaced out adequately to avoid visual clutter while providing enough detail to be informative. Use whitespace effectively to help focus attention on important areas.

- **Use Color and Shapes Strategically:** Different colors and shapes can indicate different types of information or denote relationships and hierarchies. Such visual cues enhance the map's readability and cognitive impact.
- **Align Spatially with Cognitive Load:** Place more complex or important information in the central or upper portions of the map, where they are more likely to be noticed and remembered.
- **Consistency in Layout:** Keep a consistent style in the use of lines, spacing, and symbols throughout the map to prevent confusion and maintain cognitive ease.

The visual-spatial arrangement in mind mapping is more than just an aesthetic choice; it is a critical cognitive tool that harnesses the brain's visual processing abilities. By effectively implementing this principle, mind mappers can enhance learning, recall, and problem-solving, making mind maps a powerful tool in educational, personal, and professional contexts. This principle ensures that mind maps are not only functional but also intuitively aligned with how our brains work best.

Color Coding and Imagery:

The use of colors and images not only makes mind maps more engaging but also enhances memory retention. Colors can be used to group related themes or denote different types of information, while images can help to evoke associations and make abstract concepts more concrete.

Importance of Color Coding and Imagery in Mind Mapping

Color coding and imagery transform a basic mind map into a more engaging and mentally stimulating visual tool. By integrating colors and images, mind maps tap into the brain's innate ability to process visual information, which is faster and more efficient than processing textual data. These elements help to organize information visually, making it more accessible and easier to remember.

Benefits of Color Coding and Imagery

Enhanced Memory Retention: Colors and images can act as powerful mnemonic devices. The human brain is naturally adept at recalling vivid visual and colorful information. Using distinct colors and relevant imagery in a mind map helps reinforce memory retention by creating strong associative links between visual cues and the information they represent.

Improved Focus and Interest: Colors attract the eyes and can help to differentiate between separate themes or sections within a mind map, reducing cognitive strain and focusing attention where it's most needed. Imagery, on the other hand, can make abstract concepts more concrete, sparking interest and keeping the user engaged with the content.

Faster Information Retrieval: Color coding enables quicker navigation within a mind map by allowing individuals to associate colors with specific types of information or themes. This visual distinction speeds up the process of locating information within the map, which is particularly useful in complex or densely populated mind maps.

Stimulates Creative Thinking: The use of vivid and associative imagery can stimulate creative thinking and problem-solving. Images can evoke emotions and memories, broadening the context of the ideas generated and explored in a mind map. This can lead to more innovative solutions and a deeper understanding of the mapped content.

Aids in Pattern Recognition: Different colors can highlight connections, similarities, and differences between the ideas and data within a mind map, facilitating pattern recognition and analytical thinking. This is crucial in tasks that involve sorting through complex data or identifying trends and correlations.

Implementing Color Coding and Imagery Effectively

To maximize the cognitive benefits of using color coding and imagery in mind maps, consider these strategies:

- **Consistent Use of Color:** Assign specific colors to specific types of information or to different themes to maintain consistency throughout the mind map. This consistency helps in forming strong mental associations and enhances the map's overall navigability.

- **Selective Imagery:** Choose images that are directly relevant to the content they represent. Overloading a mind map with unnecessary images can lead to distraction and reduce cognitive efficacy. The right image should simplify a concept or strengthen an association, not complicate it.

- **Balance Between Text and Visuals:** While images and colors are highly beneficial, they should not overwhelm the textual content. Balance is key; ensure that visual elements support and enhance the text, rather than overshadow it.

- **Adaptive Use of Visuals:** Adapt the use of colors and imagery according to the task at hand and the needs of the user. For example, in educational settings, brighter, varied colors might be more engaging for younger students, while a more subdued palette may be appropriate in professional or business contexts.

Color coding and imagery are not merely decorative aspects of mind mapping but are core principles that significantly enhance its cognitive benefits. By carefully integrating these visual elements, mind maps become more effective tools for learning, memory enhancement, creative thinking, and efficient information management. These principles ensure that mind maps are not only functional and informative but also visually stimulating and mentally engaging.

Cognitive Benefits of Mind Mapping

The design principles of mind mapping align closely with cognitive functions, offering several benefits that enhance mental performance:

1. **Enhanced Memory and Recall:** The combination of keywords, images, and color in a structured spatial layout makes mind maps highly memorable. Visual cues help to trigger associations and

recall, making mind maps particularly effective for studying and memorizing large volumes of information.

2. **Improved Learning and Comprehension:** By organizing information visually and hierarchically, mind maps mimic the natural way the brain processes information. This alignment helps users understand and retain complex concepts and relationships more effectively.

3. **Boosted Creativity and Idea Generation:** The radiant structure of mind maps encourages divergent thinking, making it an excellent tool for brainstorming sessions. The open format allows for unrestricted exploration of ideas, fostering creativity and innovation.

4. **Efficient Organization and Summary of Information:** Mind maps can distill complex information into a concise and manageable format. This capability makes them ideal for summarizing information, planning projects, or consolidating data from different sources.

5. **Enhanced Problem Solving:** By visualizing problems and their possible solutions in a mind map, individuals can more easily assess various aspects of a problem, identify connections, and devise comprehensive strategies for resolution.

The core principles and cognitive benefits of mind mapping make it a powerful tool for anyone looking to enhance their thinking, learning, and information management skills. By aligning with natural cognitive processes, mind mapping not only simplifies the organization of knowledge but also enhances memory, creativity, and analytical abilities, proving its value across educational, personal, and professional domains.

Traditional Applications in Various Fields:

Mind mapping has a broad array of applications across different domains. Its flexibility and effectiveness in organizing, visualizing, and recalling information make it an invaluable tool in education, business, and personal development.

<u>Education</u>

In educational settings, mind maps are extensively used as a study and learning tool. They help students visualize and understand the connections between different concepts, which is essential for deep learning. Applications include:

- **Note-Taking:** Mind maps can transform monotonous lecture notes into vibrant, structured diagrams that capture the core elements of lessons, making review sessions more efficient.
- **Study Aids:** By organizing revision material into mind maps, students can create powerful visual aids that enhance memory retention and make complex subjects manageable and less overwhelming.
- **Essay Planning and Writing:** Mind maps assist in structuring essays, from thesis development to conclusion, ensuring a coherent flow of ideas and comprehensive coverage of the topic.

<u>Business</u>

In the corporate world, mind mapping is used for strategic planning, project management, and innovation. Its ability to condense complex information and foster creative thinking makes it especially valuable for:

- **Meeting and Workshop Facilitation:** Mind maps can be used to plan and record the outcomes of meetings and workshops, ensuring ideas are captured and follow-ups are clear.

- **Project Planning:** Managers use mind maps to outline project phases, tasks, and dependencies, providing a clear overview for team members and stakeholders.
- **Brainstorming:** Mind mapping encourages out-of-the-box thinking and collaboration, making it an excellent tool for brainstorming sessions that aim to generate new ideas and solutions.

Personal Development

Individuals use mind mapping for personal goal setting and productivity enhancement. It serves as a reflective practice that helps people organize their thoughts and actions:

- **Goal Setting:** Mind maps can help individuals visualize their goals and the necessary steps to achieve them, enhancing motivation and clarity.
- **Life Planning:** From daily tasks to long-term life goals, mind maps can help individuals plan and organize various aspects of their lives in a visually engaging way.
- **Problem Solving:** Personal challenges can be deconstructed through mind mapping, allowing for a clear visualization of problems and potential solutions.

Research and Development

Researchers utilize mind mapping to structure complex information and data, facilitating analysis and discussion:

- **Literature Reviews:** Mind maps help researchers organize vast amounts of literature and findings, making it easier to identify trends, gaps, and connections.
- **Data Organization:** Complex data sets can be visually organized through mind maps, simplifying the interpretation and presentation of findings.

- **Idea Development:** New theories and models can be developed using mind maps, aiding in the visualization of abstract concepts and their relationships.

Health and Wellness

In the health sector, mind mapping has applications in patient education, therapy, and staff training:

- **Patient Education:** Mind maps are used to explain complex medical conditions and treatments to patients, ensuring they understand their health situations clearly.
- **Therapeutic Techniques:** Therapists sometimes use mind maps as a tool in cognitive behavioral therapy to help patients visualize and challenge their thoughts and behaviors.
- **Training Healthcare Staff:** Mind maps are effective in training healthcare professionals, helping them understand protocols and procedures at a glance.

The traditional applications of mind mapping in various fields demonstrate its wide-reaching impact and versatility. By enabling the structured visualization of information, fostering creative problem solving, and enhancing communication, mind mapping proves to be an essential tool in educational, professional, and personal contexts. Its ability to adapt to different needs and its effectiveness in organizing complex information continue to make it a valuable resource across disciplines.

Conclusion

Understanding the fundamental principles and benefits of mind mapping is crucial before delving into how AI can be integrated to enhance these processes. This foundational knowledge sets the stage for readers to fully appreciate the innovations discussed in subsequent chapters, ensuring they can apply these tools effectively in their professional and personal lives.

6

Chapter 2: Basics of Artificial Intelligence

Artificial Intelligence (AI) is a dynamic and rapidly evolving field that has significantly impacted various industries by enhancing efficiencies and opening new avenues for innovation. Understanding the basics of AI is crucial for grasping how it operates and how it can be integrated with other technologies like mind mapping.

Definition of Artificial Intelligence

Artificial Intelligence involves the development of computer systems capable of performing tasks that typically require human intelligence. These tasks include learning, reasoning, problem-solving, perception, and language understanding. AI aims to create machines that can mimic human cognitive functions and assist in decision-making processes.

Broad Definition of AI

At its core, Artificial Intelligence is the science and engineering of making intelligent machines, especially intelligent computer programs. It is related to the similar task of using computers to understand human intelligence, but AI does not have to confine itself to methods that are biologically observable. Simply put, AI is about making machines that can think and act like humans.

Key Aspects of Artificial Intelligence

1. **Learning:** AI systems have the ability to learn from data and experiences. Through processes such as data ingestion, analysis, and pattern recognition, these systems can improve their performance over time without human intervention.

2. **Reasoning:** AI can make decisions by applying logical rules to a set of data or information. This aspect of AI is crucial for applications requiring critical decision-making under uncertain conditions, such as in autonomous driving or medical diagnostics.

3. **Problem-solving:** Often linked closely with reasoning, problem-solving in AI involves finding solutions to complex problems in ways that are efficient, cost-effective, or meet a specific set of criteria. AI algorithms can sift through large sets of data to identify possible solutions faster than human beings.

4. **Perception:** AI systems can interpret the world around them by processing data from physical inputs. This can include visual perception through cameras or sensors, auditory perception via microphones, or even sensory data such as touch.

5. **Natural Language Understanding:** AI's ability to understand and generate human language through Natural Language Processing (NLP) allows it to communicate with users, perform tasks like translation, sentiment analysis, or content generation, and gain insights from large volumes of text data.

Evolution of the Definition

The definition of AI has evolved as the technology has advanced. Initially, AI research was focused on creating systems that could perform simple tasks equivalent to human capabilities. Over time, the focus has expanded to developing systems that can surpass human abilities in various specific tasks, known as "superintelligence."

AI and Its Goals

The ultimate goal of AI varies depending on the application but generally revolves around augmenting human capabilities and automating tasks. Some of the broader goals of AI include:

- **Augmenting Human Capabilities:** Enhancing what humans can do by providing tools that can think and act independently.
- **Automation:** Performing tasks without human intervention, which can lead to cost reduction and increased efficiency.
- **Improving Decision Making:** Providing insights that are derived from analyzing large sets of data that humans cannot process on their own.

The definition of Artificial Intelligence reflects its complexity and the vastness of its potential applications. It encapsulates a technology that is not merely about replicating human intelligence but enhancing and extending it in ways that redefine what machines are capable of. Understanding AI's definition helps in appreciating its role in driving innovations that can transform industries and improve daily life.

Key Concepts in AI

Machine Learning (ML):

Machine Learning is a subset of AI focusing on building systems that learn from data, identify patterns, and make decisions with minimal human intervention. ML algorithms improve their performance as they are exposed to more data over time.

What is Machine Learning?

Machine Learning is a subset of AI that empowers systems to learn from data, identify patterns, and make decisions with minimal human intervention. ML uses a variety of algorithms that automatically improve through experience by processing large sets of data. This ability to learn from and make predictions on data is what sets ML apart from traditional computing methods.

Core Mechanisms of Machine Learning

Machine Learning operates through several core mechanisms and processes:

1. **Supervised Learning:** This is the most prevalent type of machine learning, where the model learns from a labeled dataset. It involves training a model on a pre-defined set of data examples, which include an input and the corresponding output. The goal is for the model to learn to map inputs to outputs and to be able to predict the output from new inputs.

2. **Unsupervised Learning:** In contrast to supervised learning, unsupervised learning uses data that has not been labeled. The algorithms must discover the inherent structure within the data on their own. Common applications include clustering and association problems where the system tries to find patterns and relationships in the data.

3. **Reinforcement Learning:** This type of learning uses a system of rewards and penalties to compel the software agents and machines to learn the optimal behavior within a specific context. It is often used for various decision-making processes, including robotic controls, gaming, and navigation.

4. **Semi-supervised and Active Learning:** These are intermediate forms of learning that use a small amount of labeled data and a larger amount of unlabeled data. They are useful when acquiring a fully labeled dataset is expensive or impractical.

Importance of Machine Learning in AI
Machine learning is crucial for advancing AI for several reasons:

- **Scalability:** As data volumes grow, ML models can update and scale their learning without the need for human intervention, handling tasks more efficiently than humans could.

- **Adaptability:** ML models can adapt to new, unforeseen data without human redesign. They adjust their function in response to an ever-changing environment and input data.
- **Automation and Predictive Capabilities:** ML automates analytical model building and can make predictions or decisions based on data, essential for applications like market forecasting, resource optimization, and personalized recommendations.

Applications of Machine Learning

Machine learning has a wide range of applications, including but not limited to:

- **Healthcare:** ML algorithms can analyze historical health data to predict diseases, personalize treatments, and automate diagnostic processes.
- **Finance:** From fraud detection to algorithmic trading and credit scoring, ML is widely used in the finance sector to make faster and more accurate evaluations.
- **Retail:** ML enhances customer experience through personalized shopping and inventory management.
- **Autonomous Vehicles:** Self-driving cars use ML to make real-time navigation decisions.

Machine Learning stands as a cornerstone of Artificial Intelligence, significantly broadening the potential applications of AI across different industries. Its ability to learn from data and improve over time without human input represents a leap forward in how computers can be used to solve complex problems, make predictions, and automate tasks. As such, understanding ML is crucial for anyone engaged in or studying AI technologies.

Deep Learning:

Deep Learning is a specialized subset of ML that uses neural networks with many layers (deep neural networks) to analyze various factors of data. It excels in tasks such as image recognition, speech recognition, and natural language processing.

What is Deep Learning?

Deep Learning is a branch of machine learning that employs algorithms known as artificial neural networks. Inspired by the biological neural networks that constitute animal brains, deep learning aims to replicate this neural behavior with software, allowing machines to solve complex problems even when using data that is unstructured or unlabeled.

Core Mechanisms of Deep Learning

Deep learning models are characterized by their depth; that is, the number of layers in the neural networks:

1. **Neural Networks:** At the core of deep learning are artificial neural networks, which consist of nodes (or neurons) linked together in a format that resembles the human brain. Data enters through the input layer and passes through multiple hidden layers where the processing happens through weighted connections until it reaches the output layer. Each hidden layer's job is to transform its input data into a slightly more abstract and composite representation.

2. **Activation Functions:** These are crucial for a neural network's ability to capture complexities and perform non-linear transformations, allowing it to make sense of complicated data such as images and sound.

3. **Backpropagation:** This is a method used to refine the weights of the network by calculating the gradient of the loss function (a measure of prediction error) and propagating this error backward through the network to update the weights.

4. **Forward Propagation:** This refers to the movement of input data through the layers to the output, where predictions are made based on the learned weights.

Importance of Deep Learning in AI

Deep learning has revolutionized AI in several ways:

- **Handling Unstructured Data:** Deep learning excels in managing unstructured data such as images, sound, and text, making it a foundational technology for computer vision, speech recognition, and natural language processing.
- **Feature Learning:** Unlike traditional machine learning techniques that require manual extraction of relevant features, deep learning algorithms automatically learn the features needed for classification directly from the data, improving accuracy and efficiency.
- **Scalability and Performance:** Deep learning models improve as the amount of data increases, a property known as scalability. This makes deep learning extremely effective for tasks involving big data.

Applications of Deep Learning

Deep learning has found applications in numerous areas:

Image and Video Recognition: Deep learning algorithms are at the heart of facial recognition technology, automated image tagging in social media platforms, and object recognition in autonomous vehicles.

Speech and Language Recognition: Technologies like virtual assistants (e.g., Siri, Alexa) and real-time translation services use deep learning to understand and generate human language.

Predictive Analytics: From forecasting consumer behavior to predicting the outcomes of sporting events, deep learning models provide insights that drive decision-making processes across industries.

Healthcare: Deep learning is used for diagnostic processes including the analysis of X-rays and MRI scans, and for predictive analytics in patient monitoring and

- treatment personalization.

Deep learning is a transformative technology that underpins many of the most advanced AI applications today. By mimicking the complexity of the human brain, it allows machines to perform tasks that were once thought to be the exclusive domain of human intelligence. As technology advances, the depth and scope of deep learning continue to expand, pushing the limits of what machines can learn and achieve.

Neural Networks:

Inspired by the biological neural networks that constitute animal brains, these are a series of algorithms that attempt to recognize underlying relationships in a set of data through a process that mimics the way the human brain operates.

What are Neural Networks?

Neural networks are a series of algorithms designed to recognize underlying relationships in a set of data through a process that mimics the way the human brain operates. They consist of interconnected nodes (neurons) grouped into layers: an input layer, one or more hidden layers, and an output layer. Each node in one layer connects to nodes in the next layer, and these connections have associated weights that adjust as learning progresses.

Core Components of Neural Networks

1. **Layers:**
   - **Input Layer:** Receives various forms of input data.
   - **Hidden Layers:** Perform computations and transform the input into something the output layer can use. These layers are where most of the learning happens.
   - **Output Layer:** Produces the final results or predictions based on the inputs and the transformations by the hidden layers.

2. **Neurons (Nodes):** Each neuron in a network processes the inputs it receives, and these inputs are weighted based on their

importance. The neuron then applies an activation function to determine whether and to what extent this signal should progress further through the network.

3. **Weights:** Weights are pivotal in neural networks as they adjust during training. They represent the strength of the connection between neurons, influencing how much impact the input has on the output.

4. **Bias:** Bias is a parameter used in neural networks that allows the model to adjust its output independently of its inputs, helping the model fit better with the data.

5. **Activation Functions:** These functions are crucial for introducing non-linear properties to the network, enabling it to learn and perform more complex tasks than merely acting as a linear predictor. Common activation functions include ReLU (Rectified Linear Unit), Sigmoid, and Tanh.

How Neural Networks Learn

The process of learning in neural networks involves adjusting the weights and biases based on the error in predictions, which is determined during the training phase:

- **Forward Propagation:** Data passes through the layers of the network, from input to output. Each hidden layer transforms the input using weights, biases, and activation functions.

- **Loss Calculation:** The difference between the actual output and the predicted output (loss) is calculated using a loss function. This function measures the accuracy of the prediction.

- **Backpropagation:** In this critical step, the error is sent back through the network, allowing the network to adjust the weights and biases to decrease the error. The extent of adjustment is governed by a parameter known as the learning rate.

- **Iteration and Convergence:** This process repeats over many iterations (training cycles), with the network adjusting its weights and biases each time to minimize the loss. Over time, the network converges to a state where the error is minimized across the training set.

Applications of Neural Networks

Neural networks are versatile and powerful, applicable in numerous domains such as:

- **Computer Vision:** Used for image and video recognition, facial recognition, and autonomous vehicle navigation.
- **Natural Language Processing:** Powers language translation, sentiment analysis, and chatbots.
- **Predictive Analytics:** Utilized in weather forecasting, market trend analysis, and risk assessment.
- **Healthcare:** Aids in disease diagnosis, medical image analysis, and drug discovery.

Neural networks are a foundational technology in AI, providing the basis for complex problem-solving across various industries. By mimicking the structure and functionality of the human brain, neural networks enable machines to perform highly sophisticated tasks, marking a significant leap in the capabilities of artificial intelligence systems. As research and development continue, the potential applications and improvements in neural network architectures promise even greater advancements in AI.

Natural Language Processing (NLP):

NLP is a branch of AI that deals with the interaction between computers and humans through natural language. The ultimate objective of NLP is to read, decipher, understand, and make sense of human languages in a valuable way.

What is Natural Language Processing?

NLP combines computational linguistics—rule-based modeling of human language—with statistical, machine learning, and deep learning models. These technologies enable the processing and analysis of large amounts of natural language data. The core challenge of NLP is to enable computers to understand language in the way humans do, with all its nuances and subtleties, and then respond in a way that a human can understand.

Core Mechanisms of NLP

1. **Syntax and Semantic Analysis:**
   - **Syntax:** This refers to the arrangement of words in a sentence to make grammatical sense. NLP uses syntactic analysis to assess how the natural language aligns with grammatical rules. Common techniques include parsing and tagging.
   - **Semantics:** This involves the interpretation of the meanings behind the words. NLP tries to understand the meanings at the level of words, phrases, sentences, or even larger units of text. Semantic analysis helps distinguish between the meanings of a word in different contexts.
2. **Entity Recognition:** NLP identifies entities within text, such as the names of people, places, brands, or dates. This is crucial for extracting information and understanding the relationships between entities.
3. **Sentiment Analysis:** This involves analyzing text to determine the sentiment expressed in it. NLP algorithms detect polarity within the text (positive, negative, neutral) and are increasingly capable of detecting more nuanced emotions and opinions.
4. **Language Translation:** Automatic translation of text from one language to another is one of the most challenging aspects of NLP. This involves not only swapping words from one language to another but also retaining the correct grammatical structures, idiomatic expressions, and cultural nuances.
5. **Speech Recognition:** Translating spoken language into text is a vital NLP application. This involves algorithms that deal with

different accents, intonations, speeds of speaking, and background noises.

Importance of NLP in AI

NLP bridges the human-computer interaction gap by allowing computers to process and generate natural language in a way that is both understandable and contextually relevant to human users. Here are several ways NLP is vital in AI:

- **Enhanced User Interfaces:** NLP makes it possible for users to interact with machines using normal human language, not code or structured commands. This accessibility significantly broadens the usability of technology for non-technical users.
- **Scalable Data Analysis:** NLP techniques handle and make sense of vast volumes of text data from emails, social media, websites, and more, which would be unmanageable for humans alone.
- **Improved Customer Experience:** By automating customer service through chatbots and other AI systems, NLP can provide more immediate, accessible, and 24/7 customer support.

Applications of NLP

NLP is used in various applications that require an understanding of human language, including:

- **Chatbots and Virtual Assistants:** Tools like Siri, Alexa, and Google Assistant use NLP to understand user commands and respond in a human-like manner.
- **Content Recommendations:** NLP helps in recommending relevant articles, movies, and products to users based on the natural language content they have previously interacted with.
- **Market Intelligence:** NLP analyzes customer feedback, product reviews, and social media conversations to provide businesses with insights into public sentiment and emerging trends.

Natural Language Processing stands as a beacon in AI, showcasing its potential to bridge human and machine understanding. Through its advanced algorithms and techniques, NLP has become indispensable in various sectors, enhancing communication between humans and machines and providing deeper insights into the vast unstructured data created by human interactions. As NLP technologies continue to evolve, they promise to further revolutionize how we interact with digital systems, making those interactions more natural, intuitive, and efficient.

Computer Vision:

Computer vision is a field of AI that trains computers to interpret and understand the visual world. Using digital images from cameras and videos and deep learning models, machines can accurately identify and classify objects — and then react to what they "see."

What is Computer Vision?

Computer Vision is the process by which a computer can extract detailed information from digital images or videos to make decisions or perform actions. The goal is for computers to achieve a high level of understanding from visual inputs that can be compared to human visual understanding. Computer vision tasks can include methods for acquiring, processing, analyzing, and understanding digital images, and extraction of high-dimensional data from the real world to produce numerical or symbolic information.

Core Mechanisms of Computer Vision

1. **Image Acquisition:** This is the process of capturing and digitizing images through cameras and sensors. High-quality image acquisition is fundamental to effective computer vision.

2. **Pre-processing:** Once images are acquired, they often need to be processed to enhance image features for easier analysis. This can involve tasks such as resizing, noise reduction, and color correction.

3. **Feature Extraction:** This step involves identifying and using specific characteristics of the image, such as edges, textures, or shapes. These features help in differentiating one object from another and are crucial for the next steps of analysis.

4. **Object Detection and Recognition:** Detection identifies the presence and location of certain objects within an image, and recognition classifies them into one of the learned categories. Advanced deep learning models, particularly convolutional neural networks (CNNs), are extensively used for these tasks.

5. **Segmentation:** Image segmentation divides a visual input into segments to simplify or change the representation of an image into something that is more meaningful and easier to analyze. It is used in tasks like medical imaging to isolate regions of interest.

6. **Image Classification:** This involves assigning a label to an entire image or to specific objects within it. Classification algorithms typically use pre-labeled examples to understand the visual content of new images.

Importance of Computer Vision in AI

Computer vision is a transformative technology with the ability to impact numerous fields significantly:

- **Automated Inspection:** Computer vision systems are used in manufacturing for quality control. They can inspect products faster and with greater accuracy than human workers.

- **Surveillance:** Advanced monitoring systems use computer vision to enhance security through activities like automatic number plate recognition or monitoring crowded areas.

- **Healthcare:** In medical fields, computer vision techniques assist in diagnosing diseases by analyzing medical images, enhancing the accuracy and efficiency of treatments.

- **Automotive Industry:** Self-driving cars use computer vision to navigate and avoid obstacles. Vision systems analyze the environment and make split-second decisions that mimic human judgment.

- **Retail:** From analyzing customer behavior through video to automating checkout processes, computer vision is enhancing the shopping experience and operational efficiency.

Applications of Computer Vision

The practical applications of computer vision are vast and growing:

- **Facial Recognition:** Used for both security purposes and user authentication in personal devices.
- **Augmented Reality:** Computer vision is crucial in superimposing digital images onto the real world in AR applications.
- **Agriculture:** Automated systems for monitoring crop health and growth, and for performing tasks such as harvesting.
- **Sports Analytics:** Providing advanced metrics through analysis of movement and plays in sports.

Computer Vision is a cornerstone of modern AI applications, bridging the gap between digital computations and human-like perception and interaction with the physical world. As the technology advances, the potential for computer vision to innovate and enhance various aspects of life and work continues to expand, making it a critical area of research and development in AI.

Types of AI

AI can be categorized based on capabilities and functionalities:

Narrow AI:

Also known as Weak AI, this type of AI is designed to perform a narrow task (e.g., facial recognition or internet searches) and is the most common form of AI in use today.

What is Narrow AI?

Narrow AI refers to artificial intelligence systems that are trained and focused to perform a single or limited group of tasks. Unlike

General AI, which would possess the ability to understand and learn any intellectual task that a human can, Narrow AI is specialized to a specific task and cannot perform beyond its set parameters or training. These AI systems do not possess consciousness, genuine understanding, or the broader cognitive abilities associated with human intelligence.

Characteristics of Narrow AI

1. **Specialized Functionality:** Narrow AI excels in specific domains where it can perform tasks such as image recognition, language translation, or data analysis with speed and accuracy surpassing human capabilities.

2. **Limited Scope:** The operations of Narrow AI are confined to a predetermined range of functions and cannot adapt to tasks beyond its programming or training data.

3. **Task-Specific Learning and Adaptation:** While Narrow AI can improve its performance over time through machine learning techniques, these improvements are strictly confined to its specific operational tasks.

4. **Lack of Generalization:** Unlike more advanced AI, Narrow AI lacks the ability to generalize knowledge across disparate domains. Each Narrow AI system is tailored to its particular task and cannot easily transfer its learning to unrelated tasks.

Applications of Narrow AI

Narrow AI is pervasive across various sectors and is often embedded in systems and devices that people interact with daily:

- **Consumer Applications:** Virtual personal assistants like Apple's Siri, Amazon's Alexa, and Google Assistant are powered by Narrow AI designed to perform tasks such as setting reminders, playing music, or providing weather updates.

- **Business and Finance:** Many financial institutions employ Narrow AI for high-frequency trading, fraud detection, customer service chatbots, and personal finance assistance.
- **Healthcare:** Narrow AI applications in healthcare include diagnostic systems, personalized medicine algorithms, and robotic surgical assistants that perform specific medical procedures with precision.
- **Automotive:** AI in driver-assistance systems, such as automatic braking, lane-keeping assist, and other safety features, represents Narrow AI designed to respond to specific driving environments and conditions.
- **Manufacturing and Logistics:** Robots in production lines that perform repetitive tasks, and sorting systems in logistics and warehousing, are examples of Narrow AI streamlining operations and increasing efficiency.

Implications of Narrow AI

The implications of Narrow AI are profound in terms of enhancing productivity, increasing efficiency, and reducing human error in many fields. However, its deployment also raises ethical concerns and regulatory challenges, particularly in terms of privacy, security, and the potential for job displacement in sectors heavily reliant on repetitive tasks.

- **Ethical Considerations:** As Narrow AI systems handle more tasks, especially those involving personal data, ethical considerations about privacy and consent become paramount.
- **Economic Impact:** The automation capabilities of Narrow AI might lead to significant shifts in the labor market, requiring a reevaluation of job roles and the education system to prepare workers for more AI-integrated industries.

Narrow AI, while limited in scope compared to the aspirational goals of General AI, plays a critical role in the current landscape of technology and industry. By excelling in specific tasks, Narrow AI continues to push the boundaries of what machines can accomplish, automating complex tasks and providing insights and functionalities that were previously unattainable. As technology progresses, the role of Narrow AI will likely expand, further intertwining with everyday activities and broadening its impact across all sectors.

General AI:

General AI, or Strong AI, refers to systems that possess the ability to perform any intellectual task that a human being can. This type of AI is still theoretical and remains a significant goal of research.

What is General AI?

General AI refers to a type of artificial intelligence that exhibits human-like intellect and the capacity for generalized understanding. This means that a General AI system can theoretically perform any task, solve any problem, and learn anything that a human can, but potentially with greater speed, accuracy, and efficiency. General AI would not only be able to replicate the multi-faceted intelligence of human beings but also have the ability to transfer knowledge across different domains without needing to be retrained.

Characteristics of General AI

1. **Adaptive Learning:** General AI systems are capable of learning from experiences and applying this knowledge to new and diverse scenarios, not limited to the specific tasks they were originally programmed to perform.

2. **Understanding and Reasoning:** Unlike Narrow AI, General AI can understand context and abstract concepts, reason through problems, and make judgments that require an in-depth understanding of the world.

3. **Cognitive Flexibility:** These systems can switch between different tasks easily and adapt their approach based on the situation, much like a human.

4. **Autonomous Decision-Making:** General AI can make decisions under uncertain conditions and take into account moral and ethical considerations, similar to human decision-making processes.

Potential Applications of General AI

The realization of General AI would have profound implications across all sectors and aspects of life. Its potential applications include:

- **Universal Digital Assistants:** Assistants that can understand and perform any task, from managing households to offering complex professional services like medical diagnosis or legal advice.

- **Scientific Research:** General AI could potentially lead to major breakthroughs by hypothesizing, experimenting, and analyzing data across all scientific domains.

- **Social and Governance Solutions:** It could be used to optimize logistical systems, manage traffic, orchestrate city planning, and even govern with an objective perspective on human needs and sustainability.

Challenges and Ethical Considerations

The development of General AI poses significant technical and ethical challenges:

- **Complexity of Development:** Creating an AI with comprehensive understanding and reasoning capabilities akin to human cognition is an immensely complex task that involves advancements not only in machine learning but also in neuroscience, cognitive science, and psychology.

- **Safety and Control:** As AGI would have the capability to outperform human intelligence, ensuring it remains safe and beneficial to humanity is a crucial concern. This includes developing robust control mechanisms to prevent unintended consequences.
- **Ethical Implications:** With capabilities that could surpass human abilities, issues such as consent, privacy, and autonomy become even more critical. There's also the potential for societal disruption, such as employment impacts and inequality, which would need to be managed.

General AI represents the frontier of AI research and development, carrying both vast potential benefits and significant risks. While still largely theoretical and subject to numerous feasibility debates, the pursuit of General AI continues to drive much of the innovation and discussion in the field of artificial intelligence. As research progresses, the ethical, social, and technical aspects of creating and managing General AI will remain central topics for developers, policymakers, and the public at large.

Superintelligent AI:

This future form of AI surpasses human intelligence across all fields, including creativity, general wisdom, and social skills.

What is Superintelligent AI?

Superintelligent AI is a theoretical form of artificial intelligence that is significantly more capable than human intelligence across all domains. This type of AI would be able to perform tasks better than human experts, possessing superior problem-solving skills, decision-making abilities, and perhaps even emotional intelligence. The concept encompasses not only an enhancement of cognitive skills but also an unprecedented ability to learn, adapt, and potentially self-improve without human oversight.

Characteristics of Superintelligent AI

1. **Autonomous Learning and Adaptation:** Unlike any current AI, a superintelligent system would be capable of independent thought, learning, and decision-making without human input. It could potentially redesign its own architecture or create better algorithms to improve itself over time.
2. **Unparalleled Cognitive Abilities:** Superintelligent AI would be able to process information more quickly and accurately than humans, solving complex problems and making decisions rapidly and effectively across various disciplines.
3. **Emotional and Social Intelligence:** Beyond raw cognitive skills, superintelligent AI might also develop sophisticated emotional intelligence, enabling it to understand and manipulate social constructs and human emotions better than human beings themselves.

Potential Applications of Superintelligent AI

If realized, superintelligent AI could transform every aspect of human life, economy, and society:

- **Scientific and Technological Innovation:** Superintelligent AI could accelerate the pace of research and development, solving complex scientific problems, from climate change to curing diseases.
- **Economic and Governance Systems:** It could optimize economic systems for efficiency and fairness and might be employed in complex decision-making processes in governance, potentially offering unbiased, optimal solutions to societal challenges.
- **Personal and Professional Assistance:** Superintelligent AI could provide personalized education, career coaching, psychological counseling, and more, tailored to individual needs.

Ethical and Safety Challenges

The prospect of superintelligent AI raises profound ethical and safety concerns:

- **Control Problem:** How can humans control an entity that is smarter and more capable than themselves? Ensuring that superintelligent AI cannot harm humans or act against their interests is a significant challenge.
- **Ethical Usage:** The potential for misuse or unintended consequences of deploying superintelligent AI is enormous. Deciding who controls this technology and how it is used will have critical moral implications.
- **Existential Risk:** Superintelligent AI might pose risks that extend to the survival of the human race. Ensuring the alignment of AI goals with human values and safety is paramount.

Superintelligent AI remains a concept more speculative and theoretical than imminent. However, its potential to cause a paradigm shift in every aspect of society makes it a critical area of study within AI research. The development of such technology carries both extraordinary potential benefits and unprecedented risks. It necessitates careful, proactive governance and robust ethical considerations to ensure that if or when superintelligent AI is developed, it can coexist with humanity beneficially and safely. As we advance in our capabilities to create more intelligent systems, the discourse around superintelligence remains crucial for guiding responsible AI development and deployment.

Practical Applications

AI technologies are implemented across various sectors:

Healthcare:

Artificial Intelligence (AI) is revolutionizing the healthcare sector by enhancing diagnostic accuracy, improving treatment efficacy, and optimizing operational efficiencies. This comprehensive overview explores how AI is being integrated into various aspects of healthcare, from patient diagnosis to management and preventive care.

AI in Diagnostics

One of the most significant contributions of AI in healthcare is in the area of diagnostics. AI algorithms are particularly adept at processing and analyzing vast amounts of medical data, including imaging and genetic information, to identify patterns that may be indicative of disease. Key applications include:

- **Medical Imaging:** AI-powered systems analyze images from MRIs, CT scans, and X-rays to detect anomalies such as tumors, fractures, or diseases like pneumonia. Tools like deep learning have significantly improved the accuracy and speed of these diagnoses, often surpassing human performance in specific tasks.
- **Pathology:** AI is used to analyze sample tissues, helping pathologists identify diseases such as cancer more accurately and quickly. This is done by automating the detection of cancerous cells in tissue samples, significantly speeding up the diagnostic process and reducing human error.

AI in Treatment

AI's role extends beyond diagnosis into the treatment phase, where it assists in creating more effective and personalized treatment plans. Applications include:

- **Treatment Personalization:** AI systems analyze data from a patient's health records along with broader medical knowledge to recommend personalized treatment protocols that are optimized for the individual's specific health condition.
- **Robotic Surgery:** AI-driven robots assist surgeons in performing precise and minimally invasive surgeries. These robots can stabilize surgical instruments to enhance surgical accuracy, reduce patient recovery time, and decrease the risk of infection.
- **Virtual Nursing Assistants:** AI-powered virtual assistants provide continuous support to patients, offering medication

reminders, monitoring patient conditions, and answering questions about their health conditions, thus reducing unnecessary hospital visits and allowing real nurses to focus on more critical cases.

AI in Management and Operations

AI also streamlines healthcare management and operational processes, improving efficiency and reducing costs:

- **Hospital Workflow Management:** AI applications optimize hospital workflows by managing patient flow, treatment schedules, and the use of medical facilities. These systems help in reducing wait times and improving patient care by ensuring resources are used efficiently.
- **Supply Chain and Inventory Management:** AI systems forecast and manage the supply of medical equipment and medications. They ensure that critical items are well-stocked and help in reducing wastage of medical supplies.

AI in Preventive Healthcare

AI is playing an increasingly prominent role in preventive healthcare by enabling early detection and ongoing management of chronic diseases:

- **Predictive Analytics:** AI tools analyze patterns in patient data to predict health risks and intervene before conditions become critical. This is particularly useful in managing chronic diseases such as diabetes and heart disease, where early intervention can prevent complications.
- **Lifestyle Management and Monitoring:** Wearable health trackers that integrate AI analyze user data to provide personalized health recommendations and alerts. They monitor vital

signs, physical activity, and other health metrics to guide users towards healthier lifestyles.

Ethical and Privacy Considerations

While AI brings numerous benefits to healthcare, it also raises significant ethical and privacy concerns:

- **Data Privacy:** The use of sensitive health data requires stringent controls to protect patient privacy and ensure data is used responsibly.
- **Bias and Fairness:** AI systems must be free from biases that can affect diagnosis and treatment outcomes. Ensuring these systems are trained on diverse data sets is critical to prevent any discriminatory practices.
- **Decision Transparency:** AI systems should be transparent in their operations, particularly when they influence patient care decisions. Healthcare providers must understand how AI recommendations are derived to appropriately trust and use AI-driven advice.

AI's integration into healthcare is transforming the landscape of medical treatment, diagnosis, management, and preventive care. As these technologies continue to advance, they promise to enhance the efficiency and effectiveness of healthcare services further. However, the deployment of AI in healthcare must be managed carefully to address ethical considerations and ensure the equitable, safe, and effective use of AI technologies in this critical sector.

Automotive:

Artificial intelligence (AI) is driving significant advancements in the automotive industry, revolutionizing how vehicles are built, operated, and integrated into the broader mobility ecosystem. From enhancing vehicle safety to enabling fully autonomous driving, AI's role in automotive technology is pivotal.

AI in Autonomous Vehicles

One of the most groundbreaking applications of AI in automotive technology is in the development and operation of autonomous vehicles (AVs):

- **Self-Driving Technology:** AI systems power the core functionalities of autonomous vehicles, including sensing, decision-making, and actuation. These systems use a combination of sensors (like cameras, LIDAR, and radar), machine learning, and complex algorithms to interpret traffic data, navigate roads, and avoid obstacles.
- **Predictive Capabilities:** AI enhances the predictive capabilities of self-driving cars, allowing them to anticipate potential hazards and adjust their driving strategies accordingly. This involves complex scenario analysis and real-time decision-making, crucial for safe navigation through varied traffic conditions.
- **Optimization of Traffic Flows:** By communicating with each other and with traffic infrastructure (vehicle-to-vehicle and vehicle-to-infrastructure communications), AI-driven cars can optimize traffic patterns, reduce congestion, and improve overall road safety.

AI for Enhanced Safety Features

AI also plays a critical role in advancing safety features within traditional and next-generation vehicles:

- **Advanced Driver-Assistance Systems (ADAS):** AI powers features such as adaptive cruise control, emergency braking, lane-keeping assistance, and more. These systems continuously learn and adapt to their environments, enhancing their effectiveness over time.
- **Driver Monitoring Systems:** AI-driven systems monitor the driver's alertness, detecting signs of fatigue or distraction and

providing alerts or taking corrective actions, such as tightening the seat belt or gently applying the brakes to refocus the driver's attention.

AI in Vehicle Manufacturing

The use of AI extends into the manufacturing processes, improving efficiency, quality, and safety:

- **Predictive Maintenance:** AI algorithms predict when machines on the production line are likely to fail or need maintenance, thereby reducing downtime and increasing productivity.
- **Quality Control:** AI systems analyze images and sensor data from the assembly line to instantly detect defects or deviations from manufacturing standards, ensuring higher quality and reducing human error.
- **Supply Chain Optimization:** AI applications forecast demand more accurately, manage inventory, and optimize supply chain logistics, leading to cost reductions and more efficient production cycles.

AI in Personalized User Experiences

AI enhances the user experience by personalizing vehicle settings and interactions based on the driver's preferences and habits:

- **In-car Personal Assistant:** Voice-activated AI assistants help drivers navigate, make calls, send messages, and manage media or other in-car settings without taking their hands off the wheel, significantly improving convenience and safety.
- **Personalized Comfort Settings:** AI can adjust seating, climate, and even lighting preferences automatically by recognizing the driver or through explicit learning of the occupants' preferences over time.

Challenges and Considerations

Despite its benefits, the integration of AI in automotive technology presents challenges that need to be addressed:

- **Security and Privacy:** As vehicles become more connected, they are more vulnerable to hacking and other cyber threats. Ensuring robust cybersecurity measures is crucial to protect users' data and control over their vehicles.
- **Regulatory Compliance:** The automotive industry must navigate complex regulatory environments designed to ensure safety and reliability. As AI technologies evolve, so too must the regulatory frameworks that govern their use.
- **Ethical Implications:** The deployment of AI in automotive applications, especially autonomous driving, raises ethical questions about decision-making in critical situations, accountability for accidents, and the impact on employment in driving-related professions.

AI's application in the automotive industry is transforming vehicles from mere modes of transport into intelligent systems capable of self-management, environment interaction, and personalization. As AI technology continues to evolve, its integration into automotive applications promises even greater enhancements in vehicle functionality, production processes, and user experiences, driving the future of mobility towards unprecedented safety and efficiency levels.

Finance:

Artificial Intelligence (AI) has profoundly impacted the financial sector, revolutionizing how companies manage finances, assess risks, interact with customers, and ensure security. AI's applications in finance are vast, enhancing accuracy, increasing efficiency, and opening new avenues for innovation.

AI in Algorithmic Trading

Algorithmic trading, which uses computer programs to trade at high speeds and volumes based on predefined criteria, has been transformed by AI:

- **Market Predictions:** AI analyzes vast amounts of market data to predict stock trends and make buy or sell decisions faster than human traders. These systems use both historical and real-time data to forecast market movements with significant accuracy.
- **High-Frequency Trading (HFT):** AI drives HFT strategies, where securities are bought and sold in fractions of seconds. AI algorithms can detect patterns and execute trades at optimal times, maximizing profits.

AI in Credit Scoring and Risk Assessment

AI enhances the accuracy and efficiency of assessing client creditworthiness and managing risk:

- **Credit Scoring:** Traditional credit scoring methods are being supplemented with AI models that analyze non-traditional data sources, such as mobile phone usage and social media activity, to provide a more comprehensive view of a borrower's creditworthiness.
- **Risk Management:** AI systems predict and manage financial risks in a dynamic environment. They analyze patterns from past data to identify potential risks, helping companies adjust their strategies in advance.

AI in Fraud Detection and Prevention

AI significantly improves the ability to detect and prevent fraudulent activities by analyzing behavior patterns and spotting anomalies:

- **Pattern Recognition:** AI algorithms monitor behavior patterns related to transactions, user logins, and network traffic. Any deviation from the norm can trigger real-time alerts and automatic blocking of suspicious activities.

- **Predictive Fraud Scoring:** AI models generate scores based on transactions' likelihood of being fraudulent. These scores help financial institutions prioritize investigations and prevent potential losses.

AI in Customer Service

AI has transformed customer service within financial services through automation and personalization:

- **Chatbots and Virtual Assistants:** AI-driven chatbots handle customer inquiries 24/7, providing instant responses to common queries. This not only improves customer experience but also frees up human agents to handle more complex issues.
- **Personalized Banking Advice:** AI analyzes individual customer data to provide personalized financial advice. It can suggest optimal savings plans, investment opportunities, or even alert customers about potential financial missteps.

AI in Regulatory Compliance and Reporting

Compliance with financial regulations is critical, and AI helps simplify this complex and resource-intensive process:

- **RegTech:** AI-driven regulatory technology automates compliance processes, ensuring that financial institutions adhere to laws and regulations efficiently and less expensively.
- **Automated Reporting:** AI systems automate the generation of reports for regulatory purposes, ensuring accuracy and timeliness. They can also predict regulatory changes by analyzing trends in regulatory data.

Challenges and Ethical Considerations

While AI brings numerous benefits to finance, it also introduces challenges that need careful management:

- **Data Privacy:** As AI systems require access to vast amounts of personal and financial data, ensuring the privacy and security of this data is paramount.
- **Bias in AI Models:** AI systems are only as good as the data they are trained on. Biased data can lead to unfair credit scoring or risk assessments, disproportionately affecting certain groups.
- **Transparency and Accountability:** Decisions made by AI systems must be transparent, especially when they affect customers' financial health. Financial institutions need to be able to explain AI-driven decisions when required.

AI's integration into the financial sector is reshaping traditional practices, enabling more precise risk management, efficient operations, and enhanced customer service. As financial institutions continue to embrace AI, they must also address the ethical and practical challenges that come with its adoption, ensuring that these advanced technologies are used responsibly and inclusively. The future of finance is one where AI plays a central role in driving innovation and maintaining integrity in a rapidly evolving marketplace.

Customer Service:

Artificial Intelligence (AI) has revolutionized the customer service landscape, enhancing the efficiency and quality of support provided to customers across various industries. From automating routine tasks to personalizing customer interactions, AI has enabled organizations to improve customer satisfaction significantly while reducing operational costs.

AI in Automated Customer Interactions

One of the most visible applications of AI in customer service is in the automation of customer interactions:

- **Chatbots and Virtual Assistants:** AI-driven chatbots and virtual assistants are now common on websites, in apps, and in messaging platforms. They handle a wide range of customer inquiries, from answering frequently asked questions to troubleshooting problems and processing transactions. These AI systems use natural language processing (NLP) to interpret customer requests and respond in a conversational manner.

- **Voice Assistants:** Beyond text-based interactions, AI is also powering voice-driven customer service solutions. These systems can understand spoken requests and provide verbal responses, offering a hands-free way for customers to interact with services and support systems.

AI for Personalization in Customer Service

AI enhances the personalization of customer interactions, which can lead to increased customer loyalty and satisfaction:

- **Customer Behavior Analysis:** AI algorithms analyze customer behavior, preferences, and previous interactions to tailor responses and recommendations. This data-driven approach allows companies to offer personalized shopping suggestions, targeted marketing messages, and proactive customer support.

- **Dynamic Response Systems:** Based on the context of interactions and the customer's history, AI systems dynamically adjust their responses or escalate issues to human agents when necessary. This ensures that customers feel understood and valued throughout their service experience.

AI in Operational Efficiency

AI significantly boosts the operational efficiency of customer service departments:

- **Predictive Customer Service:** AI can predict potential issues before they become problems for customers by analyzing usage data, customer feedback, and other indicators. This proactive approach can resolve issues before they affect a large number of customers.

- **Automation of Routine Tasks:** AI automates routine and repetitive tasks such as ticket sorting, status updates, and information retrieval. This frees up human agents to focus on more complex and sensitive customer needs, thereby increasing overall team productivity.

- **Training and Coaching:** AI tools analyze interactions between customer service representatives and customers to identify best practices and areas for improvement. This information is used to train new agents and provide ongoing coaching to existing staff, ensuring consistent service quality.

Challenges and Ethical Considerations

Despite the benefits, the integration of AI into customer service also presents several challenges and ethical considerations:

- **Privacy Concerns:** The use of AI in customer service often involves the collection and analysis of large amounts of personal data. Ensuring the privacy and security of this data is crucial to maintaining customer trust.

- **Dependency on Technology:** Over-reliance on AI systems can lead to vulnerabilities, especially if these systems go offline or malfunction. Companies must have robust contingency plans in place.

- **Loss of Human Touch:** While AI can handle many aspects of customer service, it cannot entirely replace the human touch that is often necessary for empathy, complex problem-solving, and customer satisfaction. Balancing AI automation with human interaction is key.

- **Bias in AI Systems:** AI systems are susceptible to biases present in their training data. If not carefully managed, these biases can lead to unfair treatment of certain customer groups.

AI's application in customer service is profoundly reshaping how businesses interact with their customers, offering opportunities to improve service quality while optimizing efficiency. As these technologies continue to evolve, they promise further enhancements to customer service operations. However, businesses must navigate the ethical and practical challenges carefully to fully leverage AI's potential without compromising on service quality or customer trust.

Simplified Introduction to AI:

Artificial Intelligence (AI) is a dynamic field in computer science dedicated to creating systems capable of performing tasks that would normally require human intelligence. These tasks include understanding language, recognizing patterns, solving problems, and making decisions. AI is increasingly part of our everyday lives, influencing how we interact with technology at home, work, and in our communities.

Definition of Artificial Intelligence

At its core, AI involves machines performing tasks in a way that humans would consider "smart" or intelligent. It's not just about programming a computer to follow instructions; it's about enabling computers to think and learn.

Key Terms and Concepts

1. **Machine Learning (ML):** Machine Learning is a subset of AI that provides systems the ability to automatically learn and improve from experience without being explicitly programmed. ML focuses on developing computer programs that can access data and use it to learn for themselves.

2. **Deep Learning:** A technique within Machine Learning, deep learning structures algorithms in layers to create an "artificial neural network" that can learn and make intelligent decisions on its own. Deep learning is the technology behind driverless cars, enabling them to recognize a stop sign or to distinguish a pedestrian from a lamppost.

3. **Neural Networks:** Inspired by the human brain, a neural network is a series of algorithms that attempts to recognize underlying relationships in a set of data through a process that mimics the way the human brain operates.

4. **Natural Language Processing (NLP):** NLP is a field of AI focused on the interaction between computers and humans through natural language. The ultimate goal of NLP is to read, decipher, understand, and make sense of human languages in a manner that is valuable.

5. **Computer Vision:** Computer vision is an AI field that trains computers to interpret and understand the visual world. Using digital images from cameras and videos, and deep learning models, computers can identify and classify objects, and then react to what they "see."

6. **Artificial General Intelligence (AGI):** AGI, or strong AI, refers to a type of AI that is on par with human capabilities. This means an AGI can perform any intellectual task that a human can do with the ability to learn, understand, and apply knowledge in a broad, generalized way.

7. **Supervised and Unsupervised Learning:**

    ○ **Supervised Learning:** The most common technique for training AI, where the model learns from example data that has been labeled, allowing the model to predict outcomes for unforeseen data.

    ○ **Unsupervised Learning:** A type of machine learning that uses data without historical labels. The system is not told the "right answer." The algorithm must figure out what is being shown. The goal is to explore the data and find some structure within.

8. **Ethics in AI:** As AI technologies become more prevalent, ethical considerations are increasingly important. Issues of privacy, security, fairness, and transparency are at the forefront of discussions about how AI should be deployed in society.

Understanding the basics of AI involves not just knowing definitions, but also grasping how these technologies are shaping the technological landscape. From simplifying tasks and personalizing experiences to transforming industries, AI's integration into daily life is profound. As we continue to explore AI's potential, the conversation around its ethical, social, and cultural implications grows, ensuring that AI develops in a way that benefits all of humanity.

Overview Of AI's Role in Analyzing Data:

Artificial Intelligence (AI) has become an integral tool in extracting insights from data, recognizing complex patterns, and enhancing decision-making processes across various industries. By leveraging advanced algorithms and computational power, AI transforms large volumes of data into actionable intelligence.

AI in Data Analysis

Data analysis involves processing and examining data to extract useful information, draw conclusions, and support decision-making. AI significantly enhances this process:

- **Automated Data Processing:** AI can handle and analyze data at a scale and speed far beyond human capabilities. This includes cleaning data, handling missing values, and preparing datasets for analysis, which are often time-consuming when done manually.

- **Complex Data Interpretation:** AI models, especially those employing machine learning techniques, can analyze complex datasets with many variables to identify trends, correlations, and outliers. This capability is invaluable in fields like finance, healthcare, and marketing, where decisions rely on multifaceted data insights.
- **Predictive Analytics:** AI excels in developing predictive models. It can forecast future trends based on historical data, helping industries from retail to real estate to anticipate market movements, consumer behavior, and potential risks.

AI in Pattern Recognition

Pattern recognition is a branch of machine learning that focuses on the recognition of patterns and regularities in data. AI systems are particularly adept at identifying patterns that are too complex for humans to notice:

- **Image and Speech Recognition:** AI technologies such as neural networks have made significant advances in recognizing and interpreting images and speech. In healthcare, AI-driven image recognition is used to diagnose diseases from medical imaging scans with high accuracy. In consumer electronics, speech recognition powers virtual assistants like Siri and Alexa.
- **Financial Monitoring:** In finance, AI systems monitor trading patterns to identify anomalies that might indicate fraudulent activity or market manipulation. Similarly, AI-driven pattern recognition supports credit scoring models by identifying risk patterns in borrower behavior.
- **Biometric Identification:** AI-powered biometric systems use pattern recognition to enhance security through facial recognition, fingerprint identification, and other biometric markers.

AI in Decision-Making

AI enhances decision-making by providing comprehensive, accurate, and timely insights:

- **Data-Driven Decisions:** By integrating AI with big data technologies, organizations can leverage vast amounts of information to make informed decisions. AI models provide insights that help leaders choose strategies based on data rather than intuition or incomplete information.
- **Real-Time Decision Making:** In environments where time is critical, such as in high-frequency trading or emergency response, AI systems can make or suggest decisions much faster than humans can, often in real-time.
- **Risk Assessment and Management:** AI systems assess potential risks and their impacts, helping businesses manage and mitigate risks effectively. In supply chain management, for example, AI predicts and manages risks associated with inventory levels, supplier performance, and logistics.
- **Optimization:** AI algorithms are used to optimize business operations and resources, improving efficiency and productivity. For instance, AI can schedule flights, staff shifts, or deliveries in the most efficient manner, considering numerous variables and constraints.

Challenges and Ethical Considerations

While AI's role in enhancing data analysis, pattern recognition, and decision-making is transformative, it also presents challenges:

- **Bias and Fairness:** AI systems can perpetuate or even exacerbate biases if they are trained on biased data sets. Ensuring fairness and unbiased decision-making is a major concern.
- **Transparency and Explainability:** AI decisions must be transparent and explainable, especially in critical applications such as

healthcare and criminal justice. Users need to understand how decisions are made to trust and effectively use AI systems.

- **Dependency and Overreliance:** There is a risk of becoming overly dependent on AI systems, potentially leading to a lack of human oversight where it is needed.

AI's ability to analyze complex data, recognize patterns, and enhance decision-making processes marks a significant evolution in technology's role across various sectors. As these AI systems continue to evolve, they promise even greater efficiency and smarter decision-making capabilities, provided they are developed and used with careful consideration of their ethical and societal impacts.

Ethical Considerations:

As Artificial Intelligence (AI) continues to evolve and integrate into various aspects of society, its ethical implications and the future landscape it shapes demand thorough examination and proactive management.

Ethical Considerations in AI

The deployment of AI systems raises several ethical issues that must be addressed to ensure these technologies benefit society while minimizing harm:

1. **Privacy and Surveillance:** AI's capability to collect, analyze, and store vast amounts of data can lead to significant breaches of privacy. The use of AI in surveillance systems, especially by governments and corporations, raises concerns about the erosion of personal freedoms and rights to privacy.

2. **Bias and Discrimination:** AI systems can inadvertently perpetuate, amplify, and automate biases present in their training data. This can lead to unfair treatment of individuals based on race,

gender, age, or socioeconomic status, particularly in critical areas such as employment, law enforcement, and lending.

3. **Accountability and Transparency:** Determining who is responsible when AI systems make mistakes can be challenging, especially when these errors lead to accidents or legal issues. Moreover, AI algorithms often operate as "black boxes" with decision-making processes that are not transparent, making it difficult for users to understand how decisions are made.

4. **Job Displacement:** AI and automation are expected to transform various industries, potentially displacing millions of jobs. While they may also create new jobs, the net effect could be profoundly disruptive to the global workforce.

5. **Security Risks:** AI systems are vulnerable to various forms of attack, including data poisoning, model theft, and adversarial attacks, which could lead to wider social, economic, and security risks.

The Future Landscape of AI

Looking forward, the landscape of AI is set to continue its rapid evolution, affecting virtually every sector of the economy and society. Key areas of potential future development include:

1. **Proliferation of AI across Sectors:** AI will likely become ubiquitous in industries beyond technology, including agriculture, construction, and education, driving innovation and efficiency but also requiring new regulatory frameworks.

2. **Advanced Healthcare AI:** AI will play a more prominent role in diagnostics, personalized medicine, and patient care management, potentially leading to significant improvements in health outcomes and longevity.

3. **AI in Governance:** There is potential for AI to assist in public decision-making processes, improving efficiency and transparency in government operations and public services.

4. **Ethical AI Development:** As awareness of AI's ethical implications grows, there is a push towards more ethical AI development practices. This includes ensuring AI systems are fair, transparent, and built to respect user privacy and enhance security.

5. **Global AI Regulations:** The global nature of AI technology will likely necessitate international cooperation to establish standards and regulations that ensure its safe and ethical deployment worldwide.

6. **Human-AI Collaboration:** The future will increasingly see a shift from AI systems replacing human work to augmenting and collaborating with human capabilities, creating new opportunities for human-machine interaction.

The ethical considerations and the anticipated advancements in AI require careful thought, robust policy-making, and international cooperation to ensure that the benefits of AI are distributed equitably while minimizing its risks. As we stand on the brink of significant transformations brought on by AI, the need for an informed, ethical approach to its development and deployment has never been more critical. The future landscape of AI offers immense potential if navigated wisely, with a strong commitment to upholding human values and enhancing the quality of life globally.

Conclusion

The basics of Artificial Intelligence provide the groundwork for understanding how AI can be harnessed in diverse fields, including in conjunction with mind mapping to enhance cognitive and analytical capabilities. As AI technology continues to evolve, its integration into daily tools and systems is set to increase, making its study and understanding crucial for future innovations and improvements in various industries.

7

Chapter 3: The Intersection of AI and Mind Mapping

The integration of Artificial Intelligence (AI) with mind mapping techniques represents a fascinating convergence of technology and cognitive tools, enhancing how individuals and organizations conceptualize, plan, and execute tasks. This intersection enriches traditional mind mapping by introducing capabilities that extend its utility and effectiveness.

Enhancing Cognitive Processing

AI can augment the cognitive process involved in creating and utilizing mind maps:

Automated Information Synthesis:

AI can automate the synthesis of vast amounts of information into coherent and concise mind maps. For instance, AI can analyze documents, extract key concepts, and visually organize these concepts in a mind map format, saving time and improving information retention.

Concept of Automated Information Synthesis

Automated information synthesis involves using AI to process and condense large volumes of data into structured and easily understandable formats. In the context of mind mapping, AI algorithms can extract key concepts, themes, and relationships from disparate data sources—be it text documents, databases, or online content—and organize this information into a coherent mind map. This process not only speeds up the creation of mind maps but also enhances their accuracy and relevance.

Enhancing Mind Mapping with AI

1. **Data Extraction and Organization:**
    - **Extraction:** AI systems employ natural language processing (NLP) techniques to read and understand text data, identifying crucial information such as dates, names, facts, and thematic statements.
    - **Organization:** After extraction, AI algorithms categorize this information based on its relevance and relationships, automatically generating a mind map that visually represents these connections.
2. **Contextual Relevance and Updating:**
    - **Contextual Analysis:** AI analyzes the context surrounding extracted data, ensuring that the information placed in the mind map reflects its proper significance and relation to other data points.
    - **Dynamic Updates:** As new information becomes available, AI can update the mind map, adding, modifying, or reorganizing nodes and branches to reflect the latest data. This keeps the mind map current and maximally useful for decision-making and analysis.
3. **Integration of Multimodal Data:**
    - AI is not limited to text; it can incorporate data from images, videos, and audio. For example, image recognition can be used to add graphical elements to a mind map,

while sentiment analysis from customer feedback videos can be used to gauge public opinion and reflect this in the mind map.

Applications and Benefits

- **Academic Research:** Researchers can utilize AI-driven mind maps to synthesize large amounts of academic papers and literature, creating comprehensive visual summaries that highlight major findings, gaps, and emerging trends.
- **Business Intelligence:** In business settings, AI can create mind maps that summarize market research, competitor analysis, and customer feedback, providing a clear overview of the business landscape and aiding strategic planning.
- **Project Management:** Project managers can benefit from AI-generated mind maps that track project progress, resources, and dependencies, updating dynamically as project parameters change.

Challenges and Considerations

While the benefits are significant, there are challenges to the widespread adoption of AI in automated information synthesis for mind mapping:

- **Accuracy of AI Interpretations:** Depending on the training data and the specificity of the AI model, there might be inaccuracies in how AI interprets and categorizes information. Continuous training and updating of AI models are essential to maintain accuracy.
- **Complexity and Overload:** AI might generate overly complex mind maps from large data sets, potentially leading to information overload. Users need to be able to customize the level of detail and complexity according to their needs.

- **Privacy and Security:** When dealing with sensitive information, ensuring that AI systems are secure and comply with data protection regulations is paramount.

Automated information synthesis via AI presents a significant advancement in the utility and functionality of mind mapping. By enhancing how data is processed, analyzed, and visualized, AI not only improves the efficiency of creating mind maps but also the depth and actionable quality of the insights they provide. As AI technologies continue to evolve, their integration into mind mapping tools is set to redefine how individuals and organizations process information and make decisions.

Pattern Recognition:

AI enhances mind maps by identifying patterns and connections that may not be immediately apparent to human users. By analyzing data relationships, AI can suggest additional links and nodes that enrich the mind map's structure and depth.

Enhancing Mind Mapping with AI-Powered Pattern Recognition

AI-powered pattern recognition transforms how information is analyzed and represented in mind maps. Here's how AI applies its capabilities to enhance pattern recognition in mind mapping:

1. **Identifying Relationships and Connections:**
   - **Complex Data Sets:** AI algorithms analyze large and complex datasets to identify hidden patterns and relationships between data points. These patterns could relate to trends, correlations, or clusters that are not easily discernible by human analysis.
   - **Visualization Enhancements:** Once identified, these relationships are visually represented in mind maps, making the abstract connections tangible and easier to understand. AI can dynamically adjust the mind map's structure to

best represent these patterns, helping users navigate and interpret the information efficiently.

2. **Automated Categorization and Clustering:**
   - **Categorization:** AI classifies information into thematic or logical groups based on inherent similarities and differences within the data. This categorization helps in organizing the mind map into clearly defined sections or branches, improving cognitive load management.
   - **Clustering:** For more abstract data sets, AI uses clustering algorithms to group similar items, even when these groups are not explicitly labeled. This process is particularly useful in exploratory data analysis, where predefined categories might not be available.

3. **Sequential Pattern Recognition:**
   - **Temporal Data:** AI excels in recognizing patterns over time, which is crucial for data sets involving sequences or progressions, such as historical timelines, project stages, or developmental phases in education or business processes.
   - **Predictive Insights:** By recognizing these sequences, AI can not only map current data but also predict future trends or potential outcomes, which are then integrated into the mind map for strategic planning and decision-making.

Applications and Benefits

- **Business Analytics:** Companies can use AI-enhanced mind maps for market analysis, customer behavior studies, and competitive analysis, where pattern recognition helps in identifying market trends and consumer preferences.
- **Educational Learning:** Educators and students can leverage AI-driven mind maps to identify learning patterns, understand

complex scientific concepts, or organize historical events and their interconnections in a more digestible format.

- **Healthcare Data Management:** In healthcare, pattern recognition can help map patient data, treatment plans, and disease progression, aiding medical professionals in diagnosis and treatment planning.

Challenges and Considerations

While the integration of pattern recognition in mind mapping offers numerous advantages, it also presents challenges that need to be addressed:

- **Data Quality and Integrity:** The accuracy of patterns recognized by AI largely depends on the quality and completeness of the data fed into the system. Poor data quality can lead to incorrect or misleading patterns being recognized and represented in the mind maps.
- **Overfitting and Noise:** AI systems might overfit to the noise in the data, recognizing patterns that do not have statistical significance or practical applicability. This can lead to cluttered or confusing mind maps.
- **Interpretability:** There is a need for balance between automated pattern recognition and human judgment. Users must critically interpret and validate the patterns and connections that AI identifies, ensuring they are meaningful and actionable.

The integration of AI-powered pattern recognition into mind mapping tools significantly enhances their functionality, turning them into dynamic platforms for exploring and understanding complex datasets. This combination not only aids in visual learning and data analysis but also empowers decision-makers to foresee potential developments and plan accordingly. As AI technology advances, its application in mind mapping is expected to become more sophisticated, offering even greater insights and efficiencies.

Dynamic Updates:

With AI, mind maps can evolve in real-time as new information becomes available. This dynamic capability ensures that mind maps remain relevant and can adapt to include new insights or data, making them invaluable for project management and continuous learning.

AI-Driven Dynamic Updates in Mind Mapping

Dynamic updates powered by AI involve the automatic modification and refinement of mind maps based on new data inputs, changes in existing data, or shifts in project dynamics. Here's how AI facilitates these updates:

1. **Real-Time Data Integration:**
   - **Data Feeds:** AI systems can integrate and process data from various sources in real-time, including databases, sensors, and online feeds. When new data arrives, AI algorithms analyze and categorize it, automatically updating the mind map to include relevant information.
   - **Continuous Learning:** As AI systems receive new data, they not only update the mind maps but also refine their understanding of the relationships and hierarchies within the data. This ongoing learning process ensures that the mind maps become increasingly accurate and useful over time.

2. **Automated Reconfiguration:**
   - **Node and Link Adjustments:** Based on new data or changes in the project scope, AI can add, remove, or modify nodes and links in the mind map. This ensures that the structure of the mind map always aligns with the most current understanding of the data.
   - **Layout Optimization:** AI can rearrange the layout of the mind map to maintain clarity and readability, even as new

information is added. This is crucial for keeping the mind map functional and user-friendly as it grows.

3. **Predictive and Proactive Updates:**
    - **Trend Analysis:** By analyzing trends over time, AI can predict future changes or needs and proactively adjust the mind map. For example, in a project management scenario, AI might predict potential bottlenecks and highlight these areas on the mind map before they impact the project.
    - **Scenario Planning:** AI can create multiple branches or versions of a mind map based on different scenarios, allowing users to explore various future possibilities and prepare for upcoming changes.

Applications and Benefits

- **Project Management:** Dynamic updates in mind maps can help project managers keep track of progress, resources, and timelines, adjusting plans as new information becomes available or as circumstances change.
- **Business Intelligence:** In business settings, mind maps updated dynamically with market data or consumer trends can provide companies with a powerful tool for strategic planning and competitive analysis.
- **Academic Research:** For researchers, dynamically updated mind maps can integrate new research findings or data sets, providing a current view of the research landscape and helping identify emerging areas of interest or gaps in knowledge.

Challenges and Considerations

While dynamic updates offer substantial benefits, they also present challenges that need careful management:

- **Complexity Management:** As mind maps grow and are dynamically updated, they can become overly complex. Users must have tools to customize the level of detail shown or to focus on specific sections of the map.
- **Data Overload:** Continuous updates can lead to information overload. Effective filters or mechanisms to highlight significant changes are necessary to ensure that users can still find value in the dynamically updated mind maps.
- **Reliance on Data Quality:** The effectiveness of dynamic updates depends heavily on the quality and reliability of the data sources. Inaccurate or incomplete data can lead to misleading updates, potentially causing confusion or incorrect decisions.

Dynamic updates powered by AI transform traditional mind mapping into a more powerful, adaptive tool that responds in real-time to changes and new information. This capability enhances decision-making, planning, and analysis across various fields by ensuring that mind maps remain an accurate and up-to-date reflection of knowledge and data landscapes. As AI technologies continue to advance, the integration of dynamic updates into mind mapping tools will likely become more sophisticated, offering even deeper insights and more robust decision support.

Improving Decision-Making

AI-driven mind maps can significantly enhance decision-making processes:

Scenario Simulation:

AI can simulate various scenarios within a mind map framework by predicting potential outcomes based on historical data and current trends. This feature allows users to visualize different strategies and their consequences, facilitating more informed decision-making.

Integrating Scenario Simulation with Mind Mapping

Scenario simulation involves using AI to create and analyze different hypothetical scenarios based on varying inputs and conditions.

When integrated with mind mapping, this technology allows for dynamic visualization of potential outcomes, making it a powerful tool for decision support:

1. **Visualizing Multiple Outcomes:**
   - **Dynamic Branching:** AI can generate various branches within a mind map to represent different scenarios. Each branch might represent a different decision path or a different set of external market conditions, with subsequent nodes showing possible outcomes.
   - **Comparative Analysis:** Users can visually compare these scenarios side-by-side within the mind map, assessing potential benefits, risks, and impacts of different choices or external factors.

2. **Data-Driven Insights:**
   - **Predictive Modeling:** AI uses historical data, current trends, and statistical models to predict the outcomes of different scenarios. These predictions are integrated into the mind map, providing data-backed insights that inform better decision-making.
   - **Real-Time Updates:** As new data becomes available, AI updates the scenarios to reflect the most current information, ensuring that decision-makers have the latest insights at their fingertips.

3. **Interactive Exploration:**
   - **User-Driven Scenarios:** Decision-makers can input different variables or choose different options within the mind map, and AI will simulate the outcomes based on these selections. This interactive process allows users to explore a wide range of possibilities and their potential consequences.
   - **Feedback Loops:** AI can also provide feedback on the feasibility and potential success of different scenarios based

on predictive analytics, helping users refine their strategies and choices.

Applications and Benefits

- **Strategic Business Planning:** Businesses can use AI-enhanced mind maps for strategic planning, exploring different market conditions, competitive strategies, and business models to find the optimal path forward.
- **Risk Management:** Organizations can simulate scenarios involving various risk factors, allowing them to visualize and plan for potential challenges before they arise, thus better managing their risk exposure.
- **Policy Development:** In public policy or corporate governance, scenario simulations can help predict the outcomes of different policy choices, aiding lawmakers and executives in making informed decisions that are likely to result in positive outcomes.

Challenges and Considerations

While scenario simulation within mind mapping offers extensive benefits, it also presents several challenges:

- **Complexity of Modeling:** Creating accurate models that can predict outcomes reliably is complex and requires deep expertise in data science and AI. Inaccurate models can lead to poor decisions based on faulty assumptions.
- **Overreliance on Technology:** There's a risk that decision-makers might rely too heavily on AI-generated scenarios, potentially overlooking intangible factors or human intuition that are not easily quantifiable.
- **Ethical and Privacy Concerns:** Scenario simulations may involve sensitive data, raising concerns about privacy and the

ethical use of predictive analytics. Ensuring compliance with data protection regulations and ethical guidelines is crucial.

Scenario simulation integrated within AI-enhanced mind maps significantly improves decision-making by providing a clear visualization of potential outcomes and enabling interactive exploration of different strategies. This powerful tool can support more informed, strategic decisions in business, governance, and beyond. As AI technology advances, the accuracy and utility of scenario simulations in mind mapping are likely to grow, offering even greater support for complex decision-making processes.

Optimization Algorithms:

AI can integrate optimization algorithms to help prioritize tasks or suggest the most efficient pathways for project completion. This application is particularly useful in complex projects with multiple interdependent elements.

AI Optimization Algorithms in Mind Mapping

Optimization algorithms are used in AI to find the best solution from a set of possible options, based on defined criteria and constraints. When integrated with mind mapping, these algorithms can:

1. **Prioritize Tasks and Resources:**
   - **Resource Allocation:** AI can analyze the resource requirements depicted in a mind map, such as time, manpower, or financial inputs, and optimize allocation to maximize efficiency and minimize waste.
   - **Task Prioritization:** AI evaluates the impact and urgency of various tasks within a mind map, automatically prioritizing them to ensure that critical paths are addressed first, thus aiding in effective project management.
2. **Path Optimization:**
   - **Critical Path Analysis:** Optimization algorithms can identify the critical path in project planning mind maps,

which includes the sequence of dependent tasks that extend the project duration. By optimizing these paths, projects can be completed faster and more efficiently.

- **Scenario Planning:** AI can simulate different pathways for achieving a goal within the mind map and use optimization techniques to suggest the most effective approach, taking into account potential roadblocks and resource constraints.

3. **Decision Support:**

- **Trade-off Analysis:** In decisions where trade-offs are necessary, AI can calculate the optimal compromise by quantifying the benefits and drawbacks of various options within the mind map. This helps in making informed decisions that align with strategic goals.
- **Outcome Prediction:** By modeling different decision outcomes in the mind map, AI can use historical data and predictive analytics to forecast the results of certain actions, guiding users towards decisions with the highest potential for success.

Applications and Benefits

- **Strategic Business Decisions:** Companies can utilize AI-enhanced mind maps for strategic planning, where optimization algorithms help in resource distribution, market entry strategies, and product development plans.
- **Operational Efficiency:** In operations management, AI-driven mind maps can optimize workflows, supply chain logistics, and production schedules to reduce costs and improve service delivery.
- **Academic and Research Planning:** Researchers can use AI to optimize their study designs, resource allocation, and publication

strategies, making the research process more efficient and directed toward impactful outcomes.

Challenges and Considerations

While AI-driven optimization algorithms provide significant advantages in decision-making, they also present challenges that must be managed:

- **Complexity and Usability:** The complexity of optimization algorithms may make them difficult for non-experts to understand and use effectively. Simplifying user interfaces and providing clear outputs and recommendations can help mitigate this issue.
- **Accuracy of Models:** The effectiveness of optimization depends on the accuracy of the models and data used. Incorrect or biased data can lead to suboptimal decisions, emphasizing the need for high-quality, accurate input data.
- **Dynamic Environments:** In rapidly changing environments, static optimization might not be sufficient. Continuous learning algorithms that can adapt to changes in real-time are necessary to maintain the relevance of the optimization results.

Optimization algorithms within AI-enhanced mind mapping tools transform how individuals and organizations make decisions by providing a systematic approach to evaluating multiple variables and scenarios. This integration not only supports more strategic and informed decision-making but also enhances efficiency and resource management across various applications. As AI technologies advance, the potential for even more sophisticated optimization solutions in mind mapping promises to further refine and enhance decision-making processes.

Risk Assessment:

By incorporating AI, mind maps can include predictive analytics to assess risks associated with certain decisions or strategies. AI can analyze external data sources to highlight potential issues before they arise, allowing users to make proactive adjustments.

AI-Enhanced Risk Assessment in Mind Mapping

Risk assessment is a critical component of decision-making, especially in environments where the outcomes are uncertain and the stakes are high. AI integrates with mind mapping to transform how risks are identified, analyzed, and mitigated:

1. **Automated Risk Identification:**
   - **Pattern Recognition:** AI algorithms scan through vast amounts of data to identify patterns that could signify potential risks. For example, in a project management mind map, AI might detect delays or bottlenecks that could jeopardize project timelines.
   - **Anomaly Detection:** AI is adept at detecting deviations from normal operations or expected results, flagging these anomalies as potential risks within the mind map.
2. **Risk Analysis and Prioritization:**
   - **Quantitative Risk Analysis:** AI quantifies risks by analyzing historical data and current conditions to forecast the likelihood and impact of different risk scenarios. These quantifications can be visualized in the mind map, allowing decision-makers to see which areas require their attention.
   - **Risk Prioritization:** AI evaluates and ranks risks based on their potential impact and the feasibility of mitigation strategies. This ranking is integrated into the mind map, helping users focus on managing the most critical risks first.
3. **Dynamic Risk Monitoring:**
   - **Real-Time Data Integration:** AI systems continually integrate and analyze new data, updating risk assessments in real-time. This dynamic capability is reflected in the mind

map, which evolves to represent the current risk landscape accurately.

- **Predictive Alerts:** AI can predict the escalation of certain risks based on emerging trends and alert decision-makers through the mind map interface, enabling proactive risk management.

Applications and Benefits

- **Project Management:** In project management, AI-enhanced mind maps help track project risks related to timelines, resource allocation, and external dependencies. This tool allows managers to anticipate potential issues and devise effective mitigation strategies.
- **Business Strategy Development:** Businesses use AI-driven risk assessment in mind maps to strategize new market entries, product launches, or corporate expansions, assessing everything from market risks to regulatory challenges.
- **Financial Planning:** Financial institutions integrate risk assessment in mind mapping for investment strategies, portfolio management, and compliance, ensuring a comprehensive view of financial exposures and their management.

Challenges and Considerations

While the integration of AI in risk assessment within mind maps offers transformative benefits, it also presents several challenges:

- **Complexity and Interpretability:** The algorithms used for risk assessment can be complex, and their findings may not always be easy for non-experts to interpret. Simplifying the presentation of risk data on mind maps can help enhance usability.
- **Data Sensitivity and Security:** Risk assessment often involves sensitive data. Ensuring the security of this data and maintaining

privacy compliance is crucial, especially when integrating real-time data feeds.

- **Dependence on Data Quality:** The accuracy of AI-driven risk assessment depends on the quality and completeness of the data used. Poor data quality can lead to inaccurate risk predictions, potentially leading to flawed decision-making.

Integrating AI with mind mapping for risk assessment provides a powerful tool for visualizing and managing risks in decision-making processes. This integration helps organizations and individuals not only to identify and assess risks but also to monitor and respond to them dynamically. As AI technology advances, its application in enhancing mind maps for risk assessment is expected to become even more sophisticated, offering deeper insights and more robust decision support.

Streamlining Collaboration

AI-enhanced mind maps can also revolutionize collaborative efforts:

Real-Time Collaboration:

AI can facilitate real-time updates across distributed teams, ensuring that all members have access to the latest version of a mind map. AI can also notify team members of changes or important additions, keeping everyone aligned and informed.

AI-Enhanced Real-Time Collaboration in Mind Mapping

Real-time collaboration through AI-augmented mind mapping tools offers a robust platform for teams to work together efficiently, regardless of physical location. Here's how AI contributes to enhancing this process:

1. **Synchronized Updates:**
   - **Simultaneous Editing:** AI systems can manage inputs from multiple users simultaneously, updating the mind map in real time. This ensures that all changes are

immediately visible to all team members, eliminating conflicts or the need for manual synchronization.

- ○ **Version Control:** AI can track changes made by different users, maintaining a history of revisions. This not only provides accountability but also allows team members to revert to previous versions if needed.

2. **Context-Aware Notifications:**

- ○ **Smart Alerts:** AI algorithms can analyze changes made to the mind map and send notifications to relevant team members when updates pertain to their work or areas of interest. This keeps everyone informed without overwhelming them with irrelevant data.

- ○ **Task-Related Updates:** AI can highlight deadlines, milestones, and dependencies within the mind map, alerting team members to upcoming tasks or changes in project timelines.

3. **Automated Coordination:**

- ○ **Resource Allocation:** AI can suggest optimal allocation of resources based on the tasks and goals defined in the mind map. This includes recommending which team members should tackle specific tasks based on their previous performance, skills, and current workload.

- ○ **Meeting Synchronization:** AI can automatically schedule meetings or discussions based on the availability of team members and critical project milestones marked on the mind map.

Applications and Benefits

- • **Project Management:** Real-time collaborative mind mapping is invaluable for project management, allowing team members to brainstorm, plan, and monitor projects together. Changes in project scope or tasks are immediately reflected and visible to all, ensuring quick adjustments and alignment.

- **Educational Group Projects:** In educational settings, students can collaborate on assignments and projects regardless of their physical location, promoting teamwork and facilitating peer learning.
- **Corporate Strategy Sessions:** Strategic planning can greatly benefit from real-time collaboration on mind maps, as it allows executives and different departments to contribute insights and adjustments dynamically during strategy sessions.

Challenges and Considerations

While AI-driven real-time collaboration in mind mapping provides numerous advantages, it also presents certain challenges:

- **Connectivity and Accessibility:** Effective real-time collaboration requires reliable internet connectivity. Any disruption can hinder synchronization and affect the collaboration experience.
- **User Interface Complexity:** As functionalities increase, the user interface of AI-enhanced mind mapping tools can become complex. Ensuring that these tools remain user-friendly and accessible to all team members is crucial.
- **Data Security:** Real-time collaboration involves sharing potentially sensitive information across networks. Ensuring robust security measures to protect data from unauthorized access is paramount.

Real-time collaboration facilitated by AI in mind mapping tools streamlines teamwork by allowing instantaneous communication and updates. This integration not only enhances the efficiency and effectiveness of collaborative efforts but also ensures that projects remain agile and responsive to changes. As technology progresses, AI's role in enhancing collaborative mind mapping tools is expected to expand, further transforming how teams interact and achieve collective goals.

Personalization:

AI algorithms can tailor mind maps to individual preferences or job roles, displaying information in ways that are most useful to each user. This personalization improves engagement and efficiency, particularly in complex, multi-stakeholder projects.

AI-Driven Personalization in Mind Mapping

Personalization through AI involves customizing the mind mapping experience to enhance user engagement and productivity. Here's how AI contributes to personalizing mind mapping for collaborative efforts:

1. **User Role Customization:**
   - **Role-Based Views:** AI can adjust the mind map display based on the user's role within a project or organization. For example, a project manager might see a comprehensive view with all project branches, while a team member might only see sections relevant to their tasks.
   - **Access Control:** AI algorithms can automatically manage permissions and access based on user roles, ensuring that sensitive information is protected and that users can only modify sections of the mind map relevant to their responsibilities.
2. **Adaptive Learning Interfaces:**
   - **Learning User Preferences:** Over time, AI can learn individual preferences for how information is displayed or interacted with in a mind map. It can automatically adjust formats, layouts, and visualization styles to match the user's favored approach.
   - **Recommendation Systems:** AI can suggest additions or modifications to the mind map based on past interactions, commonly used resources, or frequently contacted

team members, making the tool more intuitive and user-friendly.

3. **Predictive Interaction Support:**

   ○ **Task Prioritization:** Using historical data and current project metrics, AI can help prioritize tasks for users within the mind map, suggesting deadlines or prompting reviews when necessary.

   ○ **Proactive Alerts:** AI can predict potential bottlenecks or upcoming deadlines and alert users preemptively, helping to manage workflow and keep projects on track.

Applications and Benefits

- **Enhanced User Engagement:** Personalization increases user engagement by making mind maps more relevant and easier to use, which can lead to higher productivity and more effective collaboration.
- **Increased Efficiency:** By providing role-specific views and information, AI personalization helps reduce clutter and focus attention on the most pertinent aspects of a project, speeding up decision-making and task completion.
- **Improved Learning and Adaptation:** For educational environments or training sessions, AI-personalized mind maps can adjust to the learning pace and style of each student or trainee, enhancing the learning experience.

Challenges and Considerations

While personalization can significantly enhance the collaborative use of mind mapping, it also comes with challenges that need to be managed:

- **Privacy and Data Handling:** Personalizing user experiences requires collecting and analyzing personal data, which must be handled securely and in compliance with privacy regulations.
- **Complexity in Implementation:** Developing AI systems capable of accurately learning user preferences and adapting interfaces accordingly can be complex and resource-intensive.
- **Balance Between Personalization and Standardization:** Finding the right balance between personalized content and the need for standardization across a team or project is crucial. Too much personalization can lead to inconsistencies and confusion among team members.

AI-driven personalization in mind mapping tools has the potential to transform collaborative efforts by making the experience more user-centric. It enhances efficiency, engagement, and satisfaction by tailoring the tool to the needs and preferences of individual users. As AI technology advances, the sophistication and effectiveness of personalization in mind mapping are expected to improve, further enhancing collaborative productivity and innovation.

Integration with Other Tools:

AI enables seamless integration of mind maps with other software tools such as task managers, calendars, and databases. This integration can automate workflows and ensure consistency across platforms and projects.

AI-Driven Integration of Mind Mapping with Other Tools

AI enhances the capability of mind maps to function as central hubs for project management and team collaboration by integrating them with other essential software tools. Here's how AI facilitates this integration:

1. **Data Synchronization:**
   - **Real-time Updates:** AI can synchronize data between mind maps and other systems such as project management

software, CRM platforms, or ERP systems. Changes made in one tool can be instantly reflected in the mind map and vice versa, maintaining consistency across platforms.

- **Automated Data Transfer:** AI automates the import and export of data between systems, reducing manual entry errors and saving time. For example, updates to task statuses in project management tools can be automatically updated in the corresponding mind map.

2. **Contextual Tool Linking:**

- **Task-Specific Tool Access:** AI can identify the context of a node or branch within a mind map and link it to the appropriate tool. For instance, a node related to budget planning can be linked directly to financial management software.

- **Enhanced Resource Management:** AI can analyze resource allocation within a mind map and integrate with HR or resource management systems to ensure optimal distribution of workload and track availability.

3. **Collaborative Platform Integration:**

- **Communication Tools:** AI can integrate mind maps with communication platforms like Slack, Microsoft Teams, or email systems, enabling users to discuss nodes or branches directly through these channels. This facilitates quick communication and decision-making without leaving the mind map environment.

- **Meeting and Scheduling Tools:** AI can link parts of the mind map to scheduling tools to facilitate meetings based on the project timeline or milestones depicted in the map. This ensures that all team members are aligned and informed about upcoming discussions or deadlines.

Applications and Benefits

- **Project Management:** Teams can manage projects more efficiently as mind maps integrated with project management tools provide a visual overview of the project while keeping all task-related data synchronized across platforms.
- **Strategic Planning:** In strategic planning, the integration of mind maps with business intelligence and analytics tools helps in visualizing data-driven strategies and ensuring all relevant data points are considered.
- **Educational Collaborations:** In educational settings, integrating mind maps with learning management systems (LMS) can help students and educators organize and track learning materials, assignments, and feedback in a cohesive manner.

Challenges and Considerations

While integrating mind mapping with other tools offers extensive benefits, it also presents certain challenges:

- **Complexity in Implementation:** Setting up seamless integration between different tools and ensuring they work harmoniously can be technically challenging and may require substantial IT support.
- **Interoperability Issues:** Different tools may have varying data formats or APIs, which can complicate integration efforts. Ensuring interoperability across diverse platforms often requires customized solutions.
- **User Training and Adoption:** Users may need training to effectively utilize the integrated systems. Adoption can be hindered by resistance to new workflows or the complexity of the integrated system.

AI-driven integration of mind mapping tools with other digital systems transforms mind maps into powerful collaborative platforms that enhance communication, project management, and strategic planning.

By ensuring that mind maps are dynamically linked with other tools, AI not only streamlines workflows but also maximizes the effectiveness of collaborative efforts across various domains. As AI technology continues to advance, the potential for even deeper and more effective integrations is vast, promising to further enhance the capabilities of collaborative teams.

AI Augment Mind Mapping Techniques:

Artificial Intelligence (AI) is poised to revolutionize mind mapping techniques by enhancing their functionality, efficiency, and applicability across various domains. AI can augment traditional mind mapping tools by introducing automation, personalization, and advanced analytical capabilities. This section provides a detailed exploration of how AI can enhance mind mapping techniques, facilitating better information management, decision-making, and collaborative work.

Automation of Mind Map Creation

1. **Data Extraction and Organization:**
   - AI can automatically parse large volumes of text, extract key concepts, and organize these into a structured mind map. This includes pulling data from documents, emails, and even spoken language using natural language processing (NLP) techniques.
   - By recognizing patterns and hierarchies in the data, AI can suggest or automatically create connections between nodes, offering a preliminary, insightful map that users can refine and expand.
2. **Dynamic Content Updates:**
   - AI-driven mind maps can be updated in real-time as new information becomes available, ensuring that the content remains current and relevant. This is particularly beneficial in fields like project management and research, where ongoing updates are crucial.

- AI algorithms can monitor changes in project data or research findings and automatically reflect these changes in the mind map, reducing the need for manual adjustments.

Enhancing Cognitive Processing

1. **Advanced Pattern Recognition:**
   - AI can identify complex patterns and relationships within the data that might not be immediately obvious to human analysts. This capability can unveil deeper insights, hidden trends, or emerging issues, enriching the mind mapping process.
   - These patterns can be visually represented in the mind map, making complex data more accessible and understandable.
2. **Scenario Simulation and Planning:**
   - AI can simulate various future scenarios based on the data within a mind map. For example, in business strategy planning, AI can project potential outcomes of different strategic decisions, allowing planners to visualize the consequences of various actions within the mind map.

Streamlining Collaboration

1. **Real-Time Collaboration Enhancements:**
   - AI can manage and synchronize inputs from multiple users in real-time, ensuring that the mind map reflects all contributions without conflict or data loss.
   - Notifications and updates can be intelligently managed to alert users about relevant changes, guided by their interests and prior interactions with the map.
2. **Personalized User Experiences:**

- ○ AI can learn individual user preferences and adapt the mind mapping interface accordingly, enhancing user engagement and productivity.
- ○ Personalization can also extend to suggesting resources, tools, or data that might be relevant to the user's specific segment of the mind map, based on their past activities and the content of current discussions.

Integration with Other Digital Tools

1. **Seamless Tool Interoperability:**
   - ○ AI can facilitate the integration of mind maps with other software tools such as CRM systems, project management software, and data analytics platforms. This interoperability allows for a seamless flow of information across platforms, enhancing workflow efficiency.
   - ○ For instance, updates in a project management tool can automatically adjust timelines and task dependencies in a corresponding mind map, and vice versa.

Challenges and Ethical Considerations

While AI augmentation offers substantial benefits, it also presents challenges such as ensuring data privacy, managing the complexity of AI systems, and maintaining human oversight in automated processes. Ethical considerations must also be addressed, particularly concerning data bias and the transparency of AI-driven decisions.

AI's augmentation of mind mapping represents a significant advancement in how individuals and organizations can visualize and interact with information. By automating data organization, enhancing pattern recognition, enabling scenario simulations, and improving collaborative features, AI not only makes mind mapping more dynamic but also more impactful. As AI technologies evolve, their integration into mind mapping tools will likely become deeper and more sophisticated, further enhancing their utility in professional and educational contexts.

AI's Role in Automating:

Automation of Mind Maps

AI revolutionizes mind mapping by automating several aspects of the mind mapping process:

1. **Automated Creation:** AI algorithms can automatically generate mind maps from large text blocks, extracting key concepts and relationships. This is particularly useful in academic and corporate settings where large amounts of information are common. AI can parse through documents, emails, and other content to create initial mind maps that users can refine and expand as needed.

2. **Continuous Updates:** AI-enabled mind maps can dynamically update as new data becomes available. For instance, AI can integrate real-time data feeds to continuously refresh and modify the mind map, ensuring that the information remains current and relevant, which is crucial for decision-making in fast-paced environments.

3. **Content Summarization:** AI can condense lengthy content into succinct nodes and connections within mind maps, making complex information more digestible and easier to navigate. This summarization helps in reducing cognitive overload, allowing users to focus on decision-making rather than data processing.

Enhancing Organization

AI significantly improves how information is organized within mind maps:

1. **Intelligent Clustering:** By employing clustering algorithms, AI can organize related information into coherent groups within a mind map. This helps in better visualizing the relationships and hierarchies among different data points, which can lead to more insightful analyses and conclusions.

2. **Contextual Arrangement:** AI can analyze the context surrounding data points and intelligently decide their placement within the mind map. This context-aware organization aids in better understanding the information by seeing how different pieces of data relate to each other within the broader topic.

3. **Adaptive Layouts:** AI can optimize the layout of a mind map based on the user's interaction patterns and preferences. This adaptive capability ensures that the mind map remains user-friendly and efficient, even as more data is added or as the complexity of the information increases.

Enhancing Capabilities

AI extends the capabilities of mind maps beyond simple visualization:

1. **Predictive Analytics:** Integrating predictive analytics into mind maps allows for forecasting future trends and potential outcomes based on historical data and current inputs. This feature is invaluable for strategic planning and risk management, providing users with foresight and preparation tools within the familiar format of a mind map.

2. **Semantic Analysis:** Through natural language processing, AI can understand and interpret the semantics of the content included in mind maps. This deeper understanding can enhance the accuracy of the information presented and provide richer insights into the data.

3. **Interactive Elements:** AI can introduce interactive elements into mind maps, such as clickable nodes that offer detailed

information on-demand or simulation tools that allow users to explore different scenarios directly from the mind map interface.

Challenges and Ethical Considerations

Despite these benefits, the integration of AI into mind mapping tools presents challenges such as ensuring data accuracy, maintaining privacy and security of information, and managing the potential complexity of AI-enhanced mind maps. Ethical considerations must also be addressed, especially in terms of bias in automated content generation and the transparency of AI processes.

AI's role in automating, organizing, and enhancing mind maps is crucial for leveraging these tools in more advanced, data-intensive scenarios. By bringing intelligence and adaptability to mind mapping, AI not only simplifies complex data interactions but also enhances the overall utility of mind maps as decision-making tools. As AI technology continues to evolve, its integration into mind mapping is expected to deepen, offering even greater capabilities and transforming how we visualize and interact with information.

Real-World Examples and Case Studies:

The integration of Artificial Intelligence (AI) with mind mapping is revolutionizing various industries by enhancing how professionals visualize data, manage projects, and make strategic decisions

Case Study 1: Healthcare – Patient Care and Treatment Planning

Background: A large hospital network implemented AI-driven mind mapping to improve patient care coordination and treatment planning.

Implementation: AI was used to automatically generate and update mind maps based on patients' electronic health records. Each patient's mind map included medical history, symptoms, diagnostic test results, and treatment plans. AI algorithms analyzed incoming data to suggest updates and potential concerns, like drug interactions or the need for additional tests.

Outcome: The use of AI-enhanced mind maps allowed healthcare providers to quickly grasp complex patient information, leading to faster and more accurate diagnoses and personalized treatment plans. The system also improved communication between different specialists, ensuring a holistic approach to patient care.

Case Study 2: Marketing – Campaign Management and Customer Insights

Background: A marketing agency adopted AI-powered mind mapping tools to manage advertising campaigns and gather deeper customer insights.

Implementation: The mind mapping tool integrated data from various sources, including social media analytics, customer feedback, and market research. AI algorithms identified key themes, consumer sentiment, and emerging trends, organizing this information into a comprehensive mind map.

Outcome: Marketers could visualize the effectiveness of different campaign strategies at a glance and adjust tactics in real time based on AI-generated insights. The tool also helped in identifying new market opportunities and tailoring messages to specific customer segments more effectively.

Case Study 3: Education – Curriculum Development and Student Assessment

Background: A university employed AI-enhanced mind mapping to refine curriculum development and assess student learning outcomes effectively.

Implementation: AI systems analyzed academic publications, course feedback, and student performance data to help faculty update course content. Mind maps were created for each course, detailing key learning objectives, required readings, and assessment methods, with dynamic updates as new educational resources became available.

Outcome: This approach helped educators ensure that curricula were up-to-date and aligned with the latest research and industry trends. Additionally, the visual nature of the mind maps made it easier for students to understand course structures and requirements, enhancing their learning experience.

Case Study 4: Financial Services – Risk Management and Compliance

Background: A financial institution integrated AI with mind mapping to enhance its risk management processes and ensure compliance with regulatory requirements.

Implementation: The AI system aggregated data from transaction records, customer profiles, and external databases to identify potential risks such as fraud or non-compliance. This information was visualized in a mind map, highlighting relationships between different data points and flagging high-risk areas.

Outcome: The visual and interactive nature of the mind maps allowed compliance officers to quickly identify and address areas of concern, improving the institution's risk management capabilities. The system also provided predictive insights, allowing the institution to proactively address potential issues before they became problematic.

These real-world examples underscore the versatility and effectiveness of AI-enhanced mind mapping in various fields, from healthcare and marketing to education and finance. By automating data integration, enhancing pattern recognition, and facilitating dynamic updates, AI-driven mind maps have become powerful tools for organizing complex information, improving decision-making, and fostering collaboration. As AI technology continues to advance, its integration with mind mapping is expected to yield even more innovative applications, further transforming professional practices across industries.

Conclusion

The intersection of AI and mind mapping represents a significant advance in cognitive tools, combining the intuitive, visual appeal of mind maps with the powerful analytical capabilities of AI. This synergy not only enhances individual and organizational productivity but also elevates the strategic planning and execution capabilities to new heights. As AI continues to evolve, its integration with mind mapping tools is likely to become more sophisticated, making this combination an indispensable asset in information management and decision-making processes.

8

Chapter 4: AI-Enhanced Mind Mapping Tools

AI-enhanced mind mapping tools represent a significant evolution in how individuals and organizations visualize information, plan projects, and collaborate. These tools leverage Artificial Intelligence (AI) to automate data processing, enhance pattern recognition, and streamline collaboration, thereby enriching the traditional capabilities of mind maps.

Key Features of AI-Enhanced Mind Mapping Tools

1. **Automated Data Integration:**
   - AI technologies enable the seamless integration of data from multiple sources into mind maps. Whether it's pulling information from databases, emails, or live feeds, AI can automatically extract relevant data, categorize it, and place it appropriately within the mind map.

2. **Dynamic Content Updates:**
   - Unlike static mind maps, AI-enhanced tools can update content in real-time as new information becomes available. This feature is particularly valuable in fast-paced

environments where staying abreast of the latest information is crucial.

3. **Advanced Pattern Recognition:**
   - AI algorithms excel at identifying complex relationships and patterns within large data sets. In mind maps, this capability allows for the automatic generation of connections and insights, helping users to see hidden relationships and underlying themes that might not be immediately obvious.

4. **Predictive Analytics:**
   - Many AI-enhanced mind mapping tools incorporate predictive analytics, which can forecast future trends based on historical data. This feature aids in scenario planning and risk assessment, allowing users to prepare for potential future developments.

5. **Personalization and Adaptive Learning:**
   - AI can tailor the mind mapping experience to individual users' preferences and learning styles. Over time, these tools learn from user interactions to present information in the most useful and accessible way, enhancing user engagement and productivity.

6. **Collaborative Features:**
   - Enhanced by AI, mind mapping tools facilitate better collaboration through features like real-time updates, synchronized editing, and role-specific views. AI can also manage permissions and notify relevant team members of important updates or changes.

Applications Across Various Sectors

1. **Project Management:**
   - In project management, AI-enhanced mind maps can dynamically track project progress, visualize tasks, and highlight bottlenecks or dependencies. This visibility helps

project managers allocate resources efficiently and keep projects on schedule.

2. **Education and Learning:**

   ○ Educators and students use AI-enhanced mind maps for structuring curriculum content, organizing study materials, and tracking learning progress. These tools can adapt to student learning progress, providing additional resources or practice as needed.

3. **Marketing and Market Research:**

   ○ Marketing professionals utilize AI-enhanced mind maps to analyze market trends, consumer behavior, and campaign results. The ability to dynamically integrate and visualize marketing data helps in strategizing and optimizing marketing efforts.

4. **Strategic Planning and Business Analysis:**

   ○ Businesses leverage these tools for strategic planning, competitor analysis, and internal audits. The integration of AI allows for a comprehensive overview of business operations and market conditions, facilitating informed decision-making.

Challenges and Considerations

While AI-enhanced mind mapping tools offer numerous advantages, they also pose challenges:

Complexity and Usability:

As these tools become more sophisticated, ensuring they remain user-friendly is crucial. Overly complex interfaces can deter users from taking full advantage of the tool's capabilities.

While AI-enhanced mind mapping tools offer significant advantages in processing and visualizing complex data, they also introduce challenges in terms of complexity and usability. Balancing the sophisticated features powered by AI with user-friendly interfaces is crucial for ensuring that these tools are accessible and effective for all users, regardless of their technical expertise. This section explores the challenges associated with the complexity and usability of AI-enhanced mind mapping tools and discusses strategies for addressing these issues.

Challenges of Complexity and Usability

1. **Interface Overload:**

   - **Feature Density:** AI-enhanced mind mapping tools can incorporate a wide range of features such as data integration, real-time updates, predictive analytics, and personalized learning algorithms. While powerful, the inclusion of numerous features can lead to a cluttered interface that overwhelms users, particularly those who are not tech-savvy.

   - **Learning Curve:** The advanced capabilities of these tools may require users to undergo extensive training to utilize them effectively. This steep learning curve can deter adoption, particularly in environments where quick assimilation into workflow is necessary.

2. **Navigation and Interaction:**

   - **Intuitive Navigation:** As mind maps grow in complexity with the addition of AI-generated insights and data points, navigating these maps can become cumbersome. Users may find it challenging to locate specific information or understand how different parts of the mind map are interconnected.

   - **User Interaction:** Effective interaction design is critical in AI-enhanced tools. Poorly designed interaction protocols can frustrate users, especially if they feel they are battling the system to perform basic tasks.

Strategies for Enhancing Usability

1. **Simplification and Customization:**

- ○ **Customizable Interfaces:** Allowing users to customize their interfaces according to their needs and preferences can significantly enhance usability. Users could choose to see a simplified version of the mind map with the option to delve deeper into details as needed.
- ○ **Adaptive Features:** Implementing adaptive user interfaces that respond to the user's level of expertise and past interactions can help in presenting the right amount of data and features, reducing complexity for novice users while still offering advanced features to more experienced ones.

2. **User-Centric Design:**

- ○ **Iterative Design Process:** Engaging with actual users during the design process to gather feedback and iteratively refine the tool can ensure the final product is aligned with user needs and expectations.
- ○ **Clear Visual Hierarchies:** Designing mind maps with clear visual hierarchies and cues can help users navigate complex information more easily. Effective use of color, icons, and spatial arrangements can guide users' attention to the most important parts of the mind map.

3. **Comprehensive User Support and Education:**

- ○ **Onboarding Tutorials:** Providing interactive tutorials and onboarding sessions can help new users understand how to navigate and use the mind mapping tool effectively.
- ○ **Ongoing Support:** Establishing a robust support system, including help desks, user forums, and regularly updated FAQs, can assist users in overcoming usability challenges as they become familiar with the tool.

The complexity and usability of AI-enhanced mind mapping tools are significant considerations that can impact their effectiveness and adoption. By focusing on user-centric design, simplification, customization, and comprehensive user support, developers can create mind mapping tools that are both powerful and accessible to a broad user base. Addressing these challenges is essential for leveraging the full potential of AI in enhancing mind mapping practices, ensuring that these tools not only perform complex tasks but also remain intuitive and engaging for all users.

Data Privacy and Security:

Handling sensitive information within these tools requires stringent security measures to protect data integrity and comply with privacy laws.

Challenges in Data Privacy and Security

1. **Sensitive Data Exposure:**
   - **Data Collection:** AI-enhanced mind mapping tools often require access to large amounts of data, including potentially sensitive information such as personal details, proprietary business information, or confidential project details.
   - **Data Storage and Access:** The storage and management of collected data pose risks, especially if data is stored in cloud environments or accessed across multiple devices. Unauthorized access or data breaches can lead to significant privacy violations and potential financial and reputational damage.
2. **Compliance with Data Protection Regulations:**
   - **Global Standards:** Organizations must ensure that their use of AI-enhanced mind mapping tools complies with international data protection laws like GDPR in Europe, CCPA in California, and other regional regulations. These laws dictate strict guidelines on data consent, user rights, and data handling practices.
   - **Sector-Specific Regulations:** Certain industries, such as healthcare and finance, have additional regulatory

requirements for handling sensitive information, further complicating compliance efforts.

Strategies for Enhancing Data Privacy and Security

1. **Robust Data Protection Measures:**
   - **Encryption:** Employing strong encryption for data at rest and in transit can protect against unauthorized access. Encryption ensures that even if data is intercepted or accessed improperly, it remains unreadable without the appropriate decryption keys.
   - **Access Controls:** Implementing strict access controls and authentication measures ensures that only authorized personnel can access sensitive data within the mind mapping tool. This includes using multi-factor authentication and role-based access controls.
2. **Data Anonymization and Minimization:**
   - **Anonymization:** Where possible, anonymizing data used in mind mapping can help protect individual privacy. Anonymization involves removing personally identifiable information from the data set, ensuring that the individuals cannot be distinguished.
   - **Data Minimization:** Limiting the data collected and stored to only what is necessary for the specific purpose can reduce the risks associated with data breaches. This practice not only aids in compliance with data protection laws but also limits potential damage in the event of a security breach.
3. **Regular Security Audits and Compliance Checks:**
   - **Security Audits:** Regular security audits help identify vulnerabilities in the mind mapping tools and the underlying infrastructure. These audits should be conducted by

independent third parties to ensure impartiality and thoroughness.

- ○ **Compliance Audits:** Regular reviews and updates to ensure compliance with evolving data protection laws are crucial. Staying abreast of legislative changes and adjusting practices accordingly helps prevent legal issues and fines.

4. **Transparent Data Policies:**

- ○ **User Consent:** Clearly informing users about what data is collected, how it is used, and who has access to it is fundamental. Obtaining explicit consent before collecting any personal data is a key requirement under many privacy laws.
- ○ **Privacy Policies:** Maintaining transparent and easily accessible privacy policies helps build trust with users and ensures legal compliance.

While AI-enhanced mind mapping tools offer significant benefits in terms of data handling and analytical capabilities, they also bring challenges in data privacy and security that must not be overlooked. Addressing these challenges through robust security measures, strict compliance with data protection laws, and proactive privacy policies is essential for safeguarding sensitive information. By prioritizing data security and privacy, organizations can not only protect themselves against potential breaches and legal repercussions but also build trust with their users, ensuring the sustainable use of these advanced tools.

Reliance on Quality Data:

The effectiveness of AI in these tools is heavily dependent on the quality of the data fed into them. Inaccurate or biased data can lead to misleading insights and poor decision-making.

AI-Powered Mind Mapping Software and Platforms:

The integration of Artificial Intelligence (AI) into mind mapping software has led to the development of advanced tools that enhance the creation, management, and utilization of mind maps. These AI-powered platforms offer a range of features from automated data integration to dynamic visualization and real-time collaboration.

MindMeister

Features:

- **AI Assisted Idea Generation:** MindMeister uses AI to suggest ideas and themes based on the initial input provided by the user, helping to jumpstart the brainstorming process.
- **Real-Time Collaboration:** Allows multiple users to work on a single mind map simultaneously, with changes synced in real-time across all devices.
- **Integration Capabilities:** Seamlessly integrates with Meister-Task, an AI-based project management tool, enabling users to convert mind maps into actionable tasks.

Benefits:

- Enhances creative processes through AI-driven suggestions.
- Supports team collaboration and project management through seamless integration.

XMind

Features:

- **Smart Layouts:** XMind employs AI to automatically adjust the layout of the mind map as new information is added, ensuring the map remains clear and organized.

- **Theme and Structure Suggestions:** Based on the content of the mind map, AI suggests themes and structures to better organize information.
- **Advanced Filtering:** AI-enhanced filtering allows users to display only the most relevant parts of the mind map based on predefined criteria.

Benefits:

- Keeps mind maps aesthetically pleasing and logically structured, enhancing readability.
- Simplifies managing complex information through smart filtering and organizational features.

Lucidchart

Features:

- **AI-Driven Diagramming:** Lucidchart uses machine learning to recommend diagram layouts based on the type of data input, simplifying the creation process.
- **Data Visualization:** Integrates with data sources like Google Sheets and Excel, automatically updating visual elements as data changes.
- **Collaborative Workflows:** Features like group chat and commenting are powered by AI to optimize communication efficiency within the tool.

Benefits:

- Reduces the time and effort needed to create professional diagrams and mind maps.
- Facilitates real-time data-driven decision-making.

Coggle

Features:

- **Simple AI Enhancements:** Though simpler than other platforms, Coggle incorporates AI to enhance usability, such as suggesting colors or branch styles based on content type.
- **Collaboration Tools:** Offers real-time collaboration with options for simultaneous editing and change tracking.
- **Integration with Google Drive:** Coggle integrates smoothly with Google Drive, allowing for easy storage and sharing.

Benefits:

- Ideal for education and small teams due to its ease of use and straightforward AI enhancements.
- Enhances collaboration in environments familiar with Google products.

Ayoa (formerly iMindMap)

Features:

- **Task Management Integration:** Combines mind mapping with task management, enhanced by AI to predict task durations and suggest deadlines.
- **AI-Powered Workflow Automation:** Automates workflows by suggesting task assignments based on past team performance data.
- **Creative AI Tools:** Includes AI tools that help in generating new ideas and providing insights based on the mind map content.

Benefits:

- Bridges the gap between visual planning and project execution.
- Supports creative and operational processes with advanced AI functionalities.

AI-powered mind mapping tools are rapidly evolving, each offering unique features that cater to different needs, from enhancing individual creativity and productivity to supporting complex team collaborations and data-driven enterprises. As AI technology continues to improve, these platforms are expected to become even more sophisticated, providing users with increasingly intuitive and powerful tools to transform their approach to information management and decision-making.

Comparative Analysis

AI-enhanced mind mapping tools have transformed how individuals and organizations visualize and manage information. This comparative analysis focuses on several leading AI-powered mind mapping platforms, evaluating their features, usability, and integration capabilities to help users choose the tool that best fits their needs.

MindMeister

Features:

- AI-assisted idea generation helps users start and expand their maps.
- Real-time collaboration tools allow multiple users to edit maps simultaneously.

Usability:

- Known for its intuitive user interface, making it easy for beginners and experienced users alike.
- Responsive design works well on various devices, including tablets and smartphones.

Integration Capabilities:

- Integrates seamlessly with MeisterTask for task management, facilitating a smooth transition from planning to execution.
- Offers Google Drive integration and supports exporting to various formats like PDF and PNG.

XMind

Features:

- Smart layouts automatically adjust as new elements are added to the mind map.
- Offers rich content embedding, including images, videos, and links directly in the map.

Usability:

- Feature-rich interface that may require a slight learning curve for new users.
- Supports dark mode and customizable themes to enhance visual comfort.

Integration Capabilities:

- Limited integration with external platforms compared to competitors.
- Supports import and export functions from/to Word, Power-Point, PDF, and other common formats.

Lucidchart

Features:

- AI-driven diagramming with suggestions for diagram types based on input data.
- Dynamic data linking allows mind maps to update automatically as source data changes.

Usability:

- Highly customizable interface with drag-and-drop functionality that supports extensive diagram customization.
- Offers guided tutorials and an extensive knowledge base for new users.

Integration Capabilities:

- Strong integration with a wide range of apps including G Suite, Microsoft Office, Slack, and more.
- API available for custom integrations, making it highly adaptable to enterprise environments.

Coggle
Features:

- Simpler AI enhancements focus on improving user experience without overwhelming with features.
- Offers collaborative features like real-time multi-user editing and color-coded changes.

Usability:

- Extremely user-friendly, ideal for education sectors and beginners.
- Supports an unlimited image and document uploads, enhancing the richness of the mind maps.

Integration Capabilities:

- Integrates well with Google Drive for storage and management.
- Limited in terms of direct integration with other productivity tools.

Ayoa (formerly iMindMap)
Features:

- Combines mind mapping with task management enhanced by AI to predict and manage project timelines.
- Creative AI tools assist in generating new ideas and automatically categorizing them.

Usability:

- Offers a unique radial map view, which some users find more visually engaging than traditional formats.
- Includes chat and voting tools for collaborative decision-making.

Integration Capabilities:

- Integrates with Google Calendar, Evernote, and Dropbox for a more connected workflow.
- Offers export options in various formats including CSV and PDF, although it's less integrated with enterprise systems compared to Lucidchart.

The choice of an AI-enhanced mind mapping tool largely depends on specific user needs—whether simplicity and ease of use are prioritized (as with Coggle), or whether advanced features and extensive integration capabilities are required (as with Lucidchart). Users in educational settings might prefer Ayoa for its creative tools, whereas businesses needing robust project management solutions might find MindMeister or Lucidchart more suitable. Each platform offers unique strengths that cater to different aspects of mind mapping and collaboration, making them valuable tools in their own right.

Selecting The Right Tool for Different Needs

Choosing the right AI-enhanced mind mapping tool involves understanding the specific needs of your organization or personal projects and how different features of these tools can meet those requirements. Here's a guide to help you select the most appropriate AI-powered mind mapping software based on various needs and contexts.

Understanding Your Needs

1. **Project Complexity:**
   - For complex projects involving large teams or extensive data, select a tool with robust integration capabilities and advanced data management features, such as Lucidchart or MindMeister.

2. **Collaboration Requirements:**
   - If your primary need is for real-time collaboration, consider tools like MindMeister or Coggle, which offer excellent collaborative features, including chat and simultaneous editing.

3. **Integration with Other Tools:**
   - For environments where integration with existing business tools is crucial (e.g., CRM, ERP), tools like Lucidchart that offer extensive API support and pre-built integrations with business platforms are ideal.

4. **User Experience Level:**
   - If the tool is intended for users who are not very tech-savvy or for educational purposes where ease of use is

critical, simpler and more intuitive platforms like Coggle or Ayoa may be more suitable.

5. **Budget Constraints:**
   - Consider the cost-effectiveness of the tool. Some tools offer free basic versions with limited features, which can be a good starting point for small teams or individual users.

Evaluating Tool Features

1. **AI Capabilities:**
   - Assess the sophistication of the AI features. Do they automate meaningful tasks? How well does the tool's AI handle data analysis, idea generation, and updates? Tools with advanced AI features can significantly enhance productivity but might require a steeper learning curve.

2. **Data Security and Compliance:**
   - Ensure that the tool meets the necessary data security standards, especially if you handle sensitive or proprietary information. Check for compliance with regulations like GDPR if you operate in or deal with data from the European Union.

3. **Support and Training:**
   - Availability of customer support and training resources can be crucial, especially for complex tools. Look for providers that offer comprehensive documentation, tutorials, and responsive customer support.

Matching Tools to Contexts

1. **Educational Use:**
   - Tools like Ayoa and Coggle, with their user-friendly interfaces and creative functionalities, are well-suited for

educational settings, helping students and teachers organize and visualize learning material effectively.

2. **Corporate and Business Planning:**

   ○ For business environments involving strategic planning, project management, and data analysis, choose tools like Lucidchart and MindMeister, which offer extensive functionalities and integration capabilities that can align with various business processes.

3. **Creative and Brainstorming Sessions:**

   ○ If the primary use is for brainstorming and creativity, tools that offer flexible, free-form canvas options and idea suggestion features can enhance creativity. XMind and Ayoa are strong candidates here, providing visual stimulus and inspiration through their diverse mapping styles and templates.

4. **Technical and Engineering Projects:**

   ○ For technical projects that require detailed diagramming alongside traditional mind mapping, Lucidchart provides advanced diagramming tools integrated with AI features, making it suitable for engineering and IT projects.

Selecting the right AI-enhanced mind mapping tool requires a clear understanding of your needs, the features each tool offers, and how well these features align with your specific context. By considering these factors carefully, you can choose a mind mapping tool that not only meets your immediate needs but also scales with your projects and helps drive productivity and innovation.

Conclusion

AI-enhanced mind mapping tools are reshaping the landscape of data visualization and collaboration, offering dynamic, intelligent, and personalized ways to manage information and projects. As AI technology continues to evolve, these tools are expected to become even more sophisticated, further enhancing their utility and transforming cognitive and collaborative processes across industries.

9

Chapter 5: Advanced Techniques and Strategies

In various fields and industries, leveraging advanced techniques and strategies is crucial for enhancing efficiency, driving innovation, and maintaining competitive advantage. This comprehensive overview explores several key areas where advanced techniques and strategies are applied, including project management, data analysis, marketing, and more. Understanding these techniques can help organizations and professionals optimize their operations and achieve strategic goals effectively.

Project Management

1. **Agile Methodologies:**
   - Agile project management is a strategy that involves breaking projects into small, manageable units, allowing for frequent reassessment and adaptation. This approach is particularly effective in environments where requirements and goals are expected to evolve over time.

- **Techniques:** Daily stand-up meetings, sprint planning, and retrospectives are part of Agile's iterative process, enhancing collaboration and continuous improvement.

2. **Lean Project Management:**
   - Lean focuses on maximizing value through waste minimization without sacrificing productivity. It's about delivering more value with fewer resources by streamlining processes.
   - **Techniques:** Value stream mapping to identify and eliminate non-value-adding activities, and continuous improvement practices such as Kaizen.

Data Analysis and Decision Making

1. **Predictive Analytics:**
   - Using statistical algorithms and machine learning techniques to identify the likelihood of future outcomes based on historical data. It is used across industries from finance to healthcare, improving decision-making by anticipating events before they occur.
   - **Techniques:** Regression analysis, machine learning models, and data mining to predict trends and behaviors.
2. **Big Data Analytics:**
   - Involves examining large and varied data sets — or big data — to uncover hidden patterns, unknown correlations, market trends, customer preferences, and other useful business information.
   - **Techniques:** Data warehousing, cloud computing, and Hadoop are often employed to handle the scale and complexity of big data.

Marketing Strategies

1. **Content Marketing:**
   - Involves creating and distributing valuable, relevant, and consistent content to attract and retain a clearly-defined audience — and, ultimately, to drive profitable customer action.
   - **Techniques:** Blog posts, videos, and social media content that provide utility to users, improving brand visibility and engagement.

2. **SEO and SEM:**
   - Search Engine Optimization (SEO) and Search Engine Marketing (SEM) are strategies used to increase visibility in search engines either through paid or organic means.
   - **Techniques:** Keyword optimization, backlinking, and pay-per-click campaigns are essential for enhancing online presence.

Innovation and Technology Adoption

1. **Blockchain Technology:**
   - Originally devised for the digital currency, Bitcoin, the tech community is now finding other potential uses for the technology. Blockchain offers enhanced security, traceability, and transparency.
   - **Techniques:** Distributed ledgers to record transactions securely in a decentralized manner, applicable in fields such as finance, supply chain, and healthcare.

2. **Artificial Intelligence and Machine Learning:**
   - AI and ML are being used to automate complex processes, provide deep insights into data, and create new ways for humans to interact with machines.
   - **Techniques:** Neural networks for deep learning applications and natural language processing (NLP) to facilitate human-computer interactions.

Sustainability and Environmental Management

1. **Circular Economy Strategies:**
   - This concept involves minimizing waste and making the most of resources. It contrasts with a traditional linear economy, which has a 'take, make, dispose' model of production.
   - **Techniques:** Reuse, recycling, and remanufacturing in product design and business models to extend the lifecycle of resources.
2. **Green Technologies and Renewable Energy:**
   - Implementing green technologies and renewable energy sources like solar, wind, and bioenergy to promote sustainable development.
   - **Techniques:** Photovoltaic cells for solar energy, wind turbines for wind energy, and bio-reactors for converting organic materials into energy.

Use AI With Mind Mapping:

Integrating Artificial Intelligence (AI) with mind mapping tools offers a powerful approach for tackling complex problems and enhancing creativity. This combination leverages AI's data processing capabilities with the visual organization of mind mapping to streamline problem-solving processes and foster innovative thinking. Below, we explore strategies and techniques for effectively using AI with mind mapping to maximize these benefits.

Enhancing Problem Solving with AI-Enhanced Mind Mapping

1. **Automated Data Synthesis:**
   - **Technique:** Use AI to automatically gather and synthesize relevant data from various sources such as databases, academic journals, and internal reports. AI can identify and

highlight key information, trends, and patterns, which are then visually mapped out in a mind map.

- ○ **Application:** This approach is particularly useful in complex scenarios like market analysis or research and development, where vast amounts of data need to be analyzed to identify feasible solutions.

2. **Dynamic Scenario Modeling:**

- ○ **Technique:** AI can be used to create and modify scenarios dynamically within a mind map based on different inputs and assumptions. By manipulating variables, AI can simulate outcomes, allowing users to visualize potential solutions and their implications.
- ○ **Application:** This is invaluable in strategic planning and forecasting, where understanding the potential outcomes of different decisions is crucial.

Fostering Creativity through AI-Driven Mind Maps

1. **Idea Generation and Expansion:**

- ○ **Technique:** Leverage AI's capability to generate ideas based on existing data within the mind map. AI can suggest new connections or areas of exploration that may not be immediately obvious, thus expanding the creative horizon.
- ○ **Application:** Useful in brainstorming sessions where generating novel ideas is essential, such as in marketing strategy development or product innovation.

2. **Pattern Interruption and Diverse Thinking:**

- ○ **Technique:** Use AI to introduce unexpected concepts or connections within the mind map. By breaking conventional thinking patterns, AI can help users explore more diverse and creative solutions.

- ○ **Application:** Effective in industries such as creative arts, advertising, and design, where innovative and unique ideas are prized.

Integrating AI with Mind Mapping for Enhanced Collaboration

1. **Real-Time Collaborative Mind Mapping:**
   - ○ **Technique:** Utilize AI-enhanced mind mapping tools that support real-time collaboration across different locations. AI can manage and synchronize inputs from multiple collaborators, ensuring the mind map is always current and reflective of collective inputs.
   - ○ **Application:** This is beneficial for projects involving cross-functional teams where timely and synchronized input is necessary for success.
2. **Personalized Mind Maps:**
   - ○ **Technique:** Apply AI to customize mind maps according to the preferences and needs of individual users. AI can adapt the level of detail, style, and complexity based on the user's profile and past interactions with the tool.
   - ○ **Application:** Enhances user engagement and effectiveness in organizations with diverse teams, helping each member contribute more effectively.

Tools and Implementation
Selecting the Right Tools:
Choose AI-enhanced mind mapping software that offers robust AI features and integration capabilities. Tools like MindMeister, XMind, or Lucidchart are equipped with AI functionalities that support these advanced techniques.
Considerations for Choosing AI-Enhanced Mind Mapping Tools

1. **AI Integration and Capabilities:**

- **Depth of AI Features:** Evaluate whether the tool offers advanced AI functionalities such as automated data synthesis, dynamic scenario modeling, and intelligent suggestions that can enrich mind maps with insightful and actionable information.
- **Customization and Learning:** Consider whether the AI can learn from user interactions and adapt to individual or organizational preferences in mind map creation and management.

2. **Usability and Interface:**

- **User-Friendliness:** The tool should have an intuitive interface that accommodates both novice users and experienced practitioners. A steep learning curve can be a barrier to effective implementation, especially in diverse teams.
- **Customization Options:** Check for the ability to customize the interface and features according to different project needs and user preferences, which is crucial for maximizing productivity and engagement.

3. **Collaboration Features:**

- **Real-Time Collaboration:** Since collaborative input is often essential in problem-solving and creative processes, the tool should support real-time editing, comments, and sharing capabilities across teams and stakeholders.
- **Integration with Other Platforms:** Ensure the tool integrates smoothly with other business systems (like project management software, data analytics platforms, or communication tools) to streamline workflows and data consistency.

4. **Scalability and Flexibility:**

- **Handling Complex Data:** The tool must be capable of handling large and complex data sets, allowing for seamless integration and visualization of various data types within mind maps.

○ **Adaptability to Various Use Cases:** It should be versatile enough to be applicable in different contexts, whether for strategic business planning, research and development, or educational purposes.

Recommended AI-Enhanced Mind Mapping Tools

1. **MindMeister:**
   ○ Best for teams looking for extensive collaboration features combined with strong AI capabilities for brainstorming and project planning.
   ○ Offers deep integration with MeisterTask, facilitating seamless task management alongside mind mapping.

2. **XMind:**
   ○ Suitable for users who require advanced mind mapping features with robust AI-driven analytics and presentation tools.
   ○ Provides a flexible platform that can handle complex data visualization and scenario analysis effectively.

3. **Lucidchart:**
   ○ Ideal for organizations that need high-level diagramming capabilities alongside traditional mind mapping.
   ○ Features strong AI functionalities that automate diagram creation and data integration, making it suitable for technical fields such as engineering and IT.

4. **Coggle:**
   ○ A good choice for educational institutions and teams requiring a straightforward, easy-to-use tool that supports basic AI functionalities and real-time collaboration.
   ○ Integrates well with Google Drive, making it a convenient option for users entrenched in the Google ecosystem.

Implementation Tips

- **Trial and Evaluation:** Most platforms offer free trials or demo versions. Utilize these to test how well the tool fits with your team's workflow and specific project needs.
- **Training and Support:** Leverage training resources provided by the tool's company. Effective training can dramatically reduce the adoption curve and help users harness the full potential of AI-enhanced features.
- **Feedback Mechanism:** Implement a feedback mechanism to gather user experiences and challenges faced while using the tool. This feedback can guide future tool enhancements or training needs.

Choosing the right AI-enhanced mind mapping tool requires careful consideration of the tool's AI capabilities, usability, collaboration features, and scalability. By selecting a tool that aligns with specific project requirements and user needs, organizations can effectively leverage AI to enhance their problem-solving and creative processes, driving innovation and improving decision-making outcomes.

Training and Adoption:

Ensure that team members are trained on how to use AI-enhanced mind mapping tools effectively. Emphasize the benefits and demonstrate real-world applications to encourage adoption.

Developing a Training Program

1. **Identify User Needs and Skill Levels:**
   - Conduct assessments to determine the existing skill levels of all potential users. Tailor training sessions to address varying levels of proficiency, ensuring that everyone, from tech-savvy users to novices, can effectively use the new tools.
   - Understand specific job roles and how the mind mapping tool fits into each role's responsibilities, allowing for more targeted and relevant training content.

2. **Comprehensive Training Sessions:**
    - **Initial Training:** Provide comprehensive training that covers all basic functionalities as well as advanced features of the mind mapping tool. Focus on demonstrating how AI functionalities can be leveraged for typical tasks your team performs.
    - **Advanced Workshops:** For users who need to use the tool's full capabilities, offer workshops that delve into complex features, such as dynamic scenario modeling and data synthesis, showing real world applications and best practices.
3. **Use Case Examples and Hands-on Practice:**
    - Integrate real-world use cases into the training to show how the tool can solve common challenges or enhance projects. This approach helps users understand the practical benefits and encourages deeper engagement with the tool.
    - Include hands-on practice sessions within the training program, allowing users to experiment with the tool in a controlled environment with guidance available.

Facilitating Tool Adoption

1. **Integration into Workflow:**
    - Work with team leaders to integrate the mind mapping tool into existing workflows. This may involve mapping out how tasks currently performed without the tool can be enhanced or streamlined with its capabilities.
    - Identify specific projects or upcoming initiatives where the tool can be immediately beneficial and encourage its use on these projects.
2. **Support and Resources:**

- Establish a support system where users can quickly get help when they encounter issues. This could be in the form of IT support, peer champions, or direct access to vendor support.
- Develop a resource portal with tutorials, FAQs, and tips for using the mind mapping tool. Update this portal regularly as new features are released or as new use cases are developed.

3. **Feedback Loop and Continuous Improvement:**
   - Implement a feedback mechanism to collect user experiences, suggestions, and difficulties faced while using the tool. Use this feedback to refine training materials and strategies, and if necessary, to customize tool settings or features.
   - Encourage a culture of continuous learning by providing updates on new features and ongoing training sessions to help users keep up with the latest developments in AI-enhanced mind mapping.

Measuring Success

1. **Performance Metrics:**
   - Define clear metrics to measure the effectiveness of the tool in enhancing productivity, solving complex problems, and fostering creativity. These might include time saved, an increase in project outputs, or qualitative feedback on the tool's impact on creative processes.
   - Regularly review these metrics to gauge the tool's effectiveness and to identify areas where additional training or support may be required.

Training and adoption are critical components in the successful implementation of AI-enhanced mind mapping tools. By developing comprehensive training programs, integrating the tool into daily workflows, and establishing robust support systems, organizations can ensure that these advanced tools are used effectively to solve complex problems and enhance creativity across teams. This holistic approach not only maximizes the investment in new technology but also supports a culture of innovation and continuous improvement.

Combining AI with mind mapping transforms traditional problem-solving and creative processes, enabling more efficient data handling, dynamic scenario planning, and innovative thinking. By adopting these advanced techniques and strategies, individuals and organizations can tackle complex challenges more effectively and foster a culture of creativity and innovation.

Optimizing Mind Mapping Sessions

Leveraging AI insights and analytics in mind mapping sessions can significantly enhance the ability to solve complex problems and stimulate creativity. AI technologies can automate data processing, uncover hidden patterns, and generate new insights, which can be crucial in making mind mapping sessions more effective and productive. Here's a strategic approach to integrating AI capabilities into mind mapping processes, focusing on optimizing the sessions for maximum benefit.

Integrating AI Insights and Analytics

1. **Pre-Session Data Preparation:**
   - **Data Aggregation:** Use AI tools to gather and aggregate data from multiple sources relevant to the mind mapping session's objectives. This may include internal reports, market research, customer feedback, and other pertinent data.
   - **Initial Analysis:** Deploy AI algorithms to analyze the aggregated data for preliminary insights, trends, and patterns. These insights can form the basis of the mind

mapping session, ensuring that discussions are grounded in data-driven findings.

2. **Real-Time AI Analytics during Sessions:**
   - **Dynamic Data Integration:** Utilize AI tools that can integrate real-time data into the mind mapping software. This allows the mind map to evolve dynamically as new information becomes available during the session.
   - **Predictive Modelling:** Apply AI models to simulate different scenarios based on the evolving map. This can help participants visualize the potential outcomes of various strategies or decisions discussed during the session.

3. **Post-Session Analysis and Follow-Up:**
   - **Comprehensive Review:** Use AI to perform a detailed analysis of the mind map created during the session. This analysis can identify key areas of focus, potential oversights, and the most promising solutions or ideas.
   - **Actionable Insights Generation:** AI can help translate the outcomes of the mind mapping session into actionable insights and concrete steps. This includes prioritizing tasks, assigning responsibilities, and setting timelines based on the insights generated during the session.

Strategies for Enhancing Mind Mapping with AI

1. **Customized Visualization Techniques:**
   - **Adaptive Visuals:** Use AI to adapt the visualization techniques of the mind map based on the complexity of the data and the preferences of the session participants. AI can suggest different layouts or formats that might clarify complex relationships or highlight subtle patterns.
   - **Interactive Elements:** Implement interactive AI-driven elements within the mind map, such as clickable nodes that provide deeper insights or additional data layers,

enhancing the interactive experience and providing more depth.

2. **Enhanced Collaboration Tools:**

   ○ **Automated Collaboration Features:** Integrate AI-driven tools that facilitate better collaboration, such as real-time update capabilities, automated conflict resolution (when changes overlap), and smart notifications to keep all participants aligned.

   ○ **Role-Based Customization:** Use AI to customize the mind mapping interface for different roles or users, presenting information that is most relevant to each participant's functions and needs.

3. **Feedback and Iterative Improvement:**

   ○ **Session Recording and Analysis:** Utilize AI to record and analyze mind mapping sessions, providing feedback on the effectiveness of the discussions and the engagement levels of participants.

   ○ **Iterative Improvement:** Based on AI analysis, continuously refine the approach to mind mapping sessions. This includes adjusting the data inputs, the structure of the sessions, and the AI tools employed to enhance their effectiveness over time.

AI-enhanced mind mapping is a powerful approach for tackling complex problems and boosting creativity within organizations. By preparing data with AI, integrating real-time AI analytics during sessions, and employing strategic follow-up analyses, businesses can maximize the outcomes of their mind mapping efforts. These strategies ensure that mind mapping sessions are not only productive but also directly aligned with data-driven insights, leading to more informed decision-making and innovative solutions.

Tips For Personalizing AI Settings

Personalizing AI settings to align with specific individual or organizational needs is crucial to maximizing the benefits of artificial intelligence technologies. Tailoring AI functionality can enhance user experience, improve efficiency, and ensure that the technology is contributing effectively to achieving business objectives or personal goals. Here are essential tips and strategies for personalizing AI settings effectively.

Understanding User Needs and Preferences

Conduct User Surveys and Feedback Sessions:

Gather information directly from the users about their preferences, challenges, and expectations regarding the AI system. Use surveys, interviews, and feedback sessions to collect this data.

Designing User Surveys

1. **Define Objectives Clearly:**
   - Before crafting the survey, clearly define what you want to learn. This could include discovering pain points, identifying features that are underused or most valued, or understanding user satisfaction levels.

2. **Develop Targeted Questions:**
   - Create questions that are direct and specific to avoid ambiguity. Use a mix of open-ended questions for qualitative insights and closed-ended questions for quantitative analysis.
   - Include questions that probe specific aspects of AI interaction, such as ease of use, functionality effectiveness, customization needs, and suggestions for improvements.

3. **Segment Your Audience:**
   - Tailor questions to different user segments based on their roles, experience with AI, and frequency of use. This segmentation helps in understanding diverse needs and can guide more personalized AI settings.

4. Choose the Right Survey Tools:

- Select survey tools that are easy to use and accessible to all users. Tools like SurveyMonkey, Google Forms, or Microsoft Forms offer functionalities that cater to a wide range of survey designs and are easy to distribute and analyze.

Conducting Feedback Sessions

1. Schedule Regular Sessions:

- Organize feedback sessions at regular intervals and after major updates or changes to the AI system. This regularity ensures continuous engagement and keeps the feedback relevant and timely.

2. Create a Structured Format:

- Use a structured format to guide the feedback session. This might include a brief demonstration of new features, a discussion period for users to share their experiences, and a brainstorming session for suggestions.
- Employ facilitation techniques to ensure that all participants can contribute, such as using round-robin sharing or breakout groups for larger sessions.

3. Record and Analyze Feedback:

- Record feedback sessions whenever possible, subject to consent from all participants. Detailed notes or recordings will help in accurately capturing the insights shared during the sessions.
- Analyze the feedback to identify common themes, unique suggestions, and potential areas for improvement. Prioritize these based on the impact and feasibility.

Leveraging Survey and Session Insights

1. Translate Insights into Action:

- ○ Use the insights gathered from surveys and feedback sessions to make informed decisions about customizing AI settings. This might include simplifying the user interface, enhancing certain functionalities, or adding new capabilities based on user demand.
- ○ Consider creating user profiles or personas based on the feedback, which can guide personalized settings and features.

2. Communicate Changes and Updates:

- ○ Keep users informed about how their feedback is being used to shape AI developments. Communicate any changes or improvements made based on their input.
- ○ This transparency can increase user trust and satisfaction, as they see their input having a direct impact on the tool's evolution.

Conducting user surveys and feedback sessions is a critical step in personalizing AI settings to suit individual and organizational needs. These efforts not only help in tailoring the AI experience but also engage users as active participants in the AI system's evolution, enhancing overall satisfaction and effectiveness. By systematically gathering and implementing user insights, organizations can ensure that their AI tools are not just powerful but also aligned perfectly with user requirements and preferences.

Analyze Usage Patterns:

Monitor how users interact with the AI system to identify common usage patterns or potential areas for improvement. Analytics tools can provide insights into which features are used most frequently and which are underutilized.

Steps for Analyzing Usage Patterns

1. Data Collection:

- **Quantitative Data:** Collect data on how frequently users engage with various features of the AI system, duration of sessions, and sequences of actions. Tools like Google Analytics, Mixpanel, or custom logging within the AI system can capture this data effectively.
- **Qualitative Data:** Gather data on user satisfaction and usability issues through feedback tools embedded within the AI system. This can include prompts for quick ratings or options to leave comments about their experience.

2. **Identify Key Metrics:**
- Define key performance indicators (KPIs) that reflect user engagement and satisfaction. Common metrics include usage frequency, feature utilization rates, error rates, and completion rates for tasks facilitated by AI.
- These metrics can help identify what aspects of the AI system are working well and which areas may need adjustments or enhancements.

3. **Segmentation of Users:**
- Segment users based on their usage behavior, roles, or preferences. Different patterns might emerge among various groups, such as frequent users versus occasional users, or beginners versus advanced users.
- This segmentation allows for more tailored AI personalizations, enhancing the user experience for each group based on their specific interactions and needs.

4. **Pattern Analysis:**
- Use statistical analysis and machine learning algorithms to analyze the collected data. Look for trends, anomalies, or common sequences within user interactions that could indicate preferences or dissatisfaction.
- For instance, high dropout rates at certain points might indicate usability problems, while frequent use of specific

features could highlight areas where the AI is providing significant value.

Utilizing Insights from Usage Patterns

1. **Personalize User Interfaces and Experiences:**
   - Based on usage patterns, customize the user interface and workflows to better align with user behaviors. For example, if data shows that certain features are used more frequently than others, these can be made more accessible on the dashboard.
   - Personalization can also extend to adaptive learning systems within the AI that tailor content, notifications, or support according to the individual user's habits and preferences.

2. **Optimize AI Features and Functions:**
   - Refine AI algorithms based on insights from usage patterns to improve accuracy, speed, and relevance. For example, if users frequently correct or override certain AI-generated suggestions, this could signal a need for recalibrating the underlying models.
   - Enhance or develop new features that align with user needs and preferences identified through pattern analysis, ensuring that the AI continues to evolve in response to actual usage.

3. **Proactive Support and Training:**
   - Use insights from usage patterns to identify areas where users may require additional support or training. Implement targeted help resources or training modules designed to address these specific areas.
   - Proactive support can reduce frustration, improve user competence, and increase overall satisfaction with the AI system.

Analyzing usage patterns is a powerful approach to understanding how users interact with AI systems and identifying their needs and preferences. By systematically collecting and analyzing these patterns, organizations can tailor AI settings to better serve their users, enhancing the effectiveness and acceptance of AI tools. This strategic approach not only optimizes the user experience but also drives higher efficiency and productivity within AI-enhanced environments.

Identify Specific Goals and Objectives:

Clearly define what each user or department hopes to achieve with the AI system. Understanding these goals is crucial for configuring the system to support them effectively.

Establishing Clear Goals and Objectives

1. **Stakeholder Interviews:**
   - Conduct interviews with key stakeholders across different levels of the organization to gather insights about their expectations and requirements from the AI system. This includes top management who may focus on strategic goals, operational staff who may prioritize efficiency, and IT personnel who may emphasize security and integration capabilities.
   - The diversity of perspectives ensures a comprehensive understanding of organizational goals, helping to align AI functionalities accordingly.

2. **Goal-Setting Workshops:**
   - Organize workshops that bring together various stakeholders to collaboratively define and prioritize goals for the AI implementation. Use techniques such as SWOT analysis (Strengths, Weaknesses, Opportunities, Threats) or SMART criteria (Specific, Measurable, Achievable, Relevant, Time-bound) to structure the discussion and outcomes.

○ These workshops not only aid in setting practical and clear objectives but also help in securing buy-in from all parts of the organization.

3. **Review of Existing Systems and Processes:**

○ Analyze current systems and workflows to identify gaps or inefficiencies that AI can address. Understanding where the current processes are falling short provides direct insight into how AI can be leveraged to make improvements.

○ This review can highlight areas for automation, enhancement, or complete overhaul, directly tying AI capabilities to organizational needs.

Tailoring AI to Meet Defined Goals

1. **Customization of AI Features:**

- With clearly defined goals, customize AI features to directly support these objectives. For instance, if the goal is to improve customer service, focus on personalizing AI in customer interactions, enhancing response times, or providing more accurate support resolutions.
- Prioritize the development and enhancement of AI features that directly contribute to achieving the set goals, ensuring resource allocation is optimized for maximum impact.

1. **Setting Performance Metrics:**

- Establish specific metrics to measure the effectiveness of AI in achieving the identified goals. These metrics might include quantitative indicators such as time saved, reduction in errors, or improvement in customer satisfaction scores.

- Regularly monitor these metrics to evaluate AI performance and make necessary adjustments to AI settings to continuously align with organizational objectives.

1. **Feedback Loops and Continuous Improvement:**

- Implement mechanisms for continuous feedback from users to ensure that AI functionalities remain aligned with evolving goals and organizational changes. This might include regular surveys, user activity logs, or feedback sessions.
- Use this feedback to fine-tune AI settings, adapting to changes in organizational strategies or external conditions that might affect predefined goals.

Identifying specific goals and objectives is fundamental to effectively personalizing AI settings for individual users or organizations. This process ensures that AI implementations are not only aligned with the strategic direction of the organization but also equipped to deliver tangible benefits. By regularly revisiting and refining these goals, organizations can maintain a dynamic and responsive AI strategy that continues to evolve in line with their changing needs and the external environment.

Customizing AI Functionalities

1. **Adjustable User Interfaces:**
    - Enable users to customize the interface according to their preferences. This might include changing layout, colors, or the amount of data displayed at one time.
    - Provide options for users to create custom dashboards or control panels that highlight the most relevant data or features for their specific tasks.
2. **Flexible Data Handling Options:**

- Allow users to set preferences for how data is collected, analyzed, and reported. This includes options for data privacy settings, data sharing permissions, and alert settings for specific data thresholds or anomalies.
- Implement user-defined rules for data processing, such as automating specific actions when certain conditions are met.

3. **Adaptive Learning Features:**

- Utilize machine learning algorithms that adapt over time based on user interactions. This could involve the AI learning to prioritize information based on what users interact with most often.
- Provide feedback mechanisms for users to "teach" the AI system by correcting it or approving its suggestions, enhancing its learning process.

Integrating AI with Existing Systems

1. **Seamless Integration Capabilities:**

- Ensure the AI system can integrate smoothly with other tools and platforms commonly used within the organization. This might include CRM software, project management tools, or communication platforms.
- Provide APIs or customization options that allow tech teams to create bespoke integrations that meet their unique workflow needs.

2. **Custom Security Settings:**

- Offer customizable security settings that align with the organization's security policies. This could include different levels of access control, encryption options, and audit trails.

○ Allow administrators to configure these settings to balance security with usability, ensuring that protections are robust without hindering performance.

Training and Support

1. **Personalized Training Programs:**
   ○ Develop training programs tailored to the specific ways that departments or individuals use the AI system. Include practical examples that are relevant to the users' daily tasks.
   ○ Offer ongoing training and support to accommodate updates in the AI system and changes in organizational needs.
2. **Proactive Support Systems:**
   ○ Establish a support framework that users can access easily when they need help. This could include live support, AI-driven helpdesks, and user forums.
   ○ Provide comprehensive resource libraries that users can refer to for self-help, including tutorials, FAQs, and best practice guides.

Personalizing AI settings is a dynamic process that requires ongoing attention and adjustment as organizational needs evolve and AI technologies advance. By engaging with users, adapting AI functionalities to meet specific needs, and ensuring robust training and support, organizations can significantly enhance the effectiveness and satisfaction with AI systems. This tailored approach not only improves operational efficiency but also drives innovation and competitive advantage.

Conclusion

Advanced techniques and strategies across different domains are essential for addressing contemporary challenges and seizing opportunities in the modern world. By adopting and refining these strategies, professionals and organizations can ensure resilience, adaptability, and continued growth in an ever-changing global landscape.

10

Chapter 6: Implementing AI in Mind Mapping

The integration of Artificial Intelligence (AI) with mind mapping tools extends across various fields, enhancing the ability to visualize information, streamline processes, and derive insights from complex data. This interdisciplinary approach allows for tailored solutions that meet the unique needs of different sectors. Here, we explore how AI-enhanced mind mapping is implemented across diverse fields such as education, healthcare, business, and project management.

Education:

1. Enhanced Learning and Retention:

AI-powered mind maps can adapt to individual student learning styles, dynamically changing to highlight key information or simplify complex topics.

AI-Enhanced Learning through Mind Mapping

1. Personalized Learning Paths:

- **Adaptability:** AI-driven mind maps can adapt to the learning pace and style of individual students, modifying the complexity and presentation of information based on their performance and engagement levels. For instance, if a student struggles with a particular concept, the AI can offer simplified explanations or additional resources within the mind map.
- **Predictive Learning:** AI algorithms analyze student data to predict areas where they might face challenges and proactively adjust the learning content to address these potential gaps, ensuring a smoother learning journey.

2. **Interactive Content Integration:**

- **Rich Media Embedding:** AI-enhanced mind maps can incorporate interactive elements such as videos, quizzes, and hyperlinks directly within the nodes. This integration makes learning more engaging and helps students grasp complex subjects more effectively by providing multiple learning modalities.
- **Real-time Updates:** As new information becomes available or curricular changes occur, AI can automatically update the mind maps, keeping the learning content current and relevant.

Improving Retention with AI-Powered Mind Maps

1. **Reinforcement Learning:**

- **Spaced Repetition:** AI systems can implement spaced repetition techniques, scheduling reviews of previously covered material at optimal intervals within the mind map. This method is proven to enhance memory retention over time.
- **Active Recall:** Incorporating features that prompt students to recall information, such as interactive quizzes

or fill-in-the-blank tests within the mind map, helps reinforce learning and assess retention in a non-linear, engaging way.

2. **Visualization and Cognitive Engagement:**
   - **Visual Cues:** AI can design mind maps with visual cues that are known to aid memory retention, such as color coding, symbols, or images. These elements make abstract concepts more concrete and memorable.
   - **Concept Linkages:** AI enhances mind maps by creating intuitive and logical linkages between concepts, helping students understand and remember relationships and hierarchies in the information, which is crucial for complex subjects.

Implementation Strategies in Educational Settings

1. **Integration with Educational Technology:**
   - Ensure that AI-enhanced mind mapping tools integrate seamlessly with existing Learning Management Systems (LMS) and educational platforms. This integration allows for a unified learning experience where educators can track progress comprehensively.

2. **Teacher and Student Training:**
   - Provide thorough training for both teachers and students on how to use AI-enhanced mind mapping tools effectively. Emphasize creative uses of the tool in various educational contexts, from primary schooling to higher education.
   - Develop support materials and tutorials that can be easily accessed to solve common issues and inspire innovative uses of mind mapping in coursework and study practices.

3. **Feedback Loops for Continuous Improvement:**

○ Establish mechanisms for collecting feedback from both educators and students on the usability and effectiveness of the AI-enhanced mind mapping tools. Use this feedback to continually refine the tool, focusing on features that specifically enhance educational outcomes.

AI-enhanced mind mapping transforms traditional educational methodologies by making learning more personalized, interactive, and visually engaging. By implementing these AI-driven tools in educational settings, institutions can significantly improve the way information is conveyed and retained by students, ultimately leading to higher engagement, better performance, and more meaningful learning experiences.

II. Curriculum Development:

Educators use AI-enhanced mind mapping to design curricula that cover all necessary educational standards and learning objectives. AI can suggest content adjustments based on current educational trends and student performance data.

Benefits of AI-Enhanced Mind Mapping in Curriculum Development

1. **Holistic Curriculum Design:**
   ○ AI-powered mind mapping allows educators to visualize the entire curriculum layout, connecting various subjects, modules, and learning outcomes in a cohesive manner. This holistic view helps in identifying overlaps, gaps, and interconnections between different areas of the curriculum, ensuring a balanced and comprehensive educational experience.

2. **Dynamic Adaptation to Educational Standards:**
   ○ AI tools can automatically update mind maps based on changes in educational standards and benchmarks. By integrating real-time data from educational boards and

standardizing bodies, AI ensures that the curriculum remains relevant and compliant with the latest educational requirements.

Methodologies for Curriculum Development Using AI Mind Maps

1. **Mapping Core Competencies and Outcomes:**
   - Educators can use AI to map out core competencies and intended learning outcomes for each course or module. AI can suggest alignments and dependencies based on established educational theories and data from similar educational programs, optimizing learning pathways.

2. **Resource and Material Integration:**
   - AI-enhanced mind maps can link directly to resources that support each part of the curriculum, such as textbooks, scholarly articles, and multimedia content. This integration ensures that educational materials are easily accessible and aligned with the curriculum goals.

3. **Feedback and Iterative Development:**
   - Utilizing AI to collect and analyze feedback from students and educators allows for the continuous improvement of the curriculum. Mind maps can be adjusted dynamically to incorporate suggestions and resolve issues, fostering an adaptive learning environment.

Implementing AI Mind Maps in Curriculum Development

1. **Collaboration Among Stakeholders:**
   - Facilitate workshops and collaborative sessions using AI-enhanced mind maps to involve various stakeholders in the curriculum development process. These tools allow for real-time updates and contributions from different

participants, ensuring a diverse and inclusive approach to curriculum design.

2. **Training and Professional Development:**

   ○ Offer professional development sessions for educators to learn how to use AI-enhanced mind mapping tools effectively in curriculum planning and development. Tailored training can help teachers and curriculum designers maximize the potential of these tools.

3. **Monitoring and Evaluation:**

   ○ Implement monitoring systems that use AI to track the effectiveness of the curriculum against educational outcomes. Mind maps can provide visual analytics on student performance data, helping educators identify areas of the curriculum that may need adjustments or enhancements.

AI-enhanced mind mapping is a transformative tool for curriculum development in education. It supports the design of comprehensive, standards-aligned curricula that are dynamically adaptable to changes in educational requirements and feedback from the learning community. By leveraging AI in mind mapping, educational institutions can enhance curriculum planning, execution, and evaluation, ultimately leading to more effective and engaging learning experiences for students.

Healthcare:

1. **Patient Data Visualization:**

AI-driven mind maps can organize and display comprehensive patient histories, treatment plans, and possible outcomes in a visual format that is easy to understand for both healthcare providers and patients.

Benefits of AI-Enhanced Mind Mapping in Patient Data Visualization

1. **Comprehensive Patient Profiles:**
   - AI-powered mind maps can integrate diverse patient data sources, including electronic health records (EHRs), lab results, and imaging data, into a unified visual representation. This holistic view aids physicians in understanding the full spectrum of a patient's health status and medical history.
2. **Real-Time Health Monitoring:**
   - AI-driven mind maps can be updated in real-time with new data inputs such as latest test results or health metrics collected via wearable technology. This capability ensures that healthcare providers have access to the most current information, critical for ongoing patient care and emergency situations.

Methodologies for Patient Data Visualization Using AI Mind Maps

1. **Visual Encoding Techniques:**
   - Employ visual encoding techniques such as color coding, symbols, or graphs within mind maps to represent different types of data or to indicate urgency levels. For example, different colors can represent various health metrics (blood pressure, glucose levels), with changes in colors or intensities reflecting deviations from normal ranges.
2. **Interactive and Layered Information:**
   - Design mind maps to be interactive, allowing healthcare providers to click on specific nodes to dive deeper into detailed data or historical trends. Layered information design helps in managing the complexity of data without overwhelming the initial view.
3. **Predictive Insights and Recommendations:**
   - Integrate predictive analytics into the mind mapping tool to forecast potential health risks based on patterns

identified in the patient data. AI can also suggest potential treatments or preventive measures, assisting doctors in making informed decisions quickly.

Implementing AI Mind Maps for Patient Data Visualization

1. **Integration with Healthcare Systems:**

- Ensure that AI-enhanced mind mapping tools are seamlessly integrated with existing healthcare information systems like EHRs and Practice Management Systems. This integration facilitates efficient data flow and reduces the likelihood of errors in manual data entry.

1. **Privacy and Security Compliance:**

- Given the sensitive nature of patient data, it's crucial that AI-driven mind mapping tools comply with healthcare regulations such as HIPAA in the U.S. or GDPR in Europe. Implement robust security measures including data encryption, secure access controls, and audit trails.

1. **Training and User Adoption:**

- Conduct comprehensive training sessions for healthcare professionals to familiarize them with the functionalities and benefits of using AI-enhanced mind mapping tools. Tailored training can help overcome resistance and encourage widespread adoption.

1. **Continuous Feedback and Improvement:**

- Establish mechanisms to collect feedback from healthcare providers who use the mind mapping tool. Use this feedback to make iterative improvements to the tool, enhancing usability and adding functionalities that meet the evolving needs of healthcare professionals.

AI-enhanced mind mapping for patient data visualization represents a significant advancement in healthcare technology. By providing a comprehensive, real-time visual representation of patient data, these tools can improve the accuracy of diagnoses, enhance the effectiveness of treatment plans, and ultimately contribute to better patient outcomes. Implementing these tools requires careful consideration of integration, security, training, and ongoing development to ensure they meet the high standards required in healthcare environments.

II. Research and Collaboration:

In medical research, AI-enhanced mind maps facilitate the consolidation of findings from various studies, identifying patterns or gaps in research.

Enhancing Medical Research with AI-Enhanced Mind Mapping

1. **Centralized Knowledge Hub:**
   - AI-powered mind maps serve as dynamic knowledge hubs where researchers can consolidate diverse data sources, including clinical trial data, literature reviews, and real-time research updates. This centralized approach helps maintain a cohesive understanding of complex research topics.
   - By organizing data visually, AI mind maps can uncover relationships and patterns that might not be evident through traditional data analysis methods.

2. **Streamlining Data Analysis:**
   - AI algorithms integrated into mind mapping tools can automatically analyze large datasets, identifying significant trends, anomalies, or correlations. This feature accelerates the data analysis process, freeing researchers to focus more on hypothesis testing and less on data management.

- Visual representations of statistical data and AI-generated insights can help clarify complex concepts, making findings more accessible and easier to communicate.

Facilitating Collaborative Medical Projects

1. **Real-Time Collaboration Features:**
   - AI-enhanced mind mapping tools equipped with real-time collaboration capabilities allow multiple users to work on the same mind map simultaneously from different locations. This feature is invaluable for multi-institutional research projects or global health initiatives.
   - Changes made by any team member are instantly visible to all, ensuring that everyone has the latest updates and reducing the risk of redundant efforts.
2. **Role-Based Access and Contribution:**
   - Implement role-based access control within the mind mapping tool to ensure that sensitive data is protected and only accessible to authorized personnel. This feature is crucial in maintaining data integrity and compliance with privacy regulations.
   - Tailor the mind map's interface and functionalities according to user roles, optimizing usability for clinicians, researchers, administrators, etc.

Implementing AI Mind Maps for Effective Research and Collaboration

1. **Integration with Existing Systems:**
   - Seamlessly integrate AI mind mapping tools with other research and healthcare systems, such as Electronic Health Records (EHRs), Laboratory Information Management Systems (LIMS), and clinical trial management systems.

This integration ensures data consistency and enhances workflow efficiency.

2. **Training and Support:**

   ○ Provide comprehensive training for all users on how to effectively utilize AI-enhanced mind mapping tools in their research and collaborative projects. Include case studies and best practice examples to illustrate practical applications.

   ○ Establish a support system for troubleshooting and technical assistance to address any issues promptly, minimizing disruptions to research activities.

3. **Feedback Loops for Continuous Improvement:**

   ○ Create feedback mechanisms within the mind mapping tool to allow users to easily report bugs, request features, or suggest improvements. Regularly review this feedback to refine the tool and adapt it to the evolving needs of the healthcare research community.

AI-enhanced mind mapping is transforming the landscape of healthcare research and collaboration. By providing sophisticated tools for data visualization, real-time collaboration, and intelligent data analysis, AI mind maps facilitate more efficient, comprehensive, and collaborative research endeavors. For healthcare professionals and researchers, these tools not only streamline complex projects but also foster an environment of innovation and shared knowledge, ultimately driving forward the boundaries of medical science.

Business

1. **Strategic Planning and Market Analysis:**

Businesses utilize AI-driven mind maps for strategic planning, leveraging AI's ability to analyze market trends and simulate future scenarios. This aids in making informed strategic decisions.

Enhancing Strategic Planning with AI-Enhanced Mind Mapping

1. **Visualization of Strategic Goals and Objectives:**
   - AI-powered mind maps can dynamically organize and visualize a company's strategic goals, key performance indicators (KPIs), and milestones. This visual representation helps align team members and stakeholders around shared objectives, enhancing strategic coherence and focus.
   - The ability to see how different objectives interconnect within a mind map allows managers to identify synergies, potential conflicts, and dependencies more effectively.
2. **Scenario Planning and Forecasting:**
   - AI-driven mind maps enable businesses to model various strategic scenarios by manipulating different variables and predicting potential outcomes. This aids in risk assessment and helps companies prepare for various market conditions.
   - Integration with real-time data feeds allows these scenarios to be updated dynamically, providing ongoing insights as market conditions change.

Facilitating Comprehensive Market Analysis

1. **Competitor Analysis and Industry Trends:**
   - Utilize AI to automatically gather and update information on competitors and industry trends, which can be visually mapped to identify patterns and shifts in the market landscape.
   - AI can analyze large volumes of data from market reports, social media, news outlets, and financial statements,

synthesizing this information into actionable insights directly within the mind map.

2. **Customer Insights and Segmentation:**
    - AI-enhanced mind maps can integrate data from customer relationship management (CRM) systems, sales data, and market research to create detailed customer profiles and segmentation.
    - Visualizing customer segments and preferences helps businesses tailor their marketing strategies and product offerings to meet specific customer needs, enhancing targeting and personalization.

Implementing AI Mind Maps for Business Strategy and Market Analysis

1. **Integration with Business Intelligence Systems:**
    - Ensure that AI-driven mind mapping tools integrate seamlessly with existing business intelligence (BI) systems and data warehouses. This integration allows for the automatic feeding of data into mind maps, ensuring that strategic plans and market analyses are always based on the most current data available.

2. **Collaborative Strategic Workshops:**
    - Use AI-enhanced mind mapping in strategic workshops to facilitate brainstorming, discussion, and decision-making among cross-functional teams. Real-time collaboration features ensure that all participants can contribute to and edit the mind map simultaneously, regardless of their location.

3. **Training and Adoption:**
    - Provide targeted training sessions for executives, strategists, and marketing teams on how to use AI-enhanced mind mapping tools effectively. Focus on demonstrating

practical applications such as developing strategic plans, conducting SWOT analyses, and visualizing market dynamics.

○ Support the adoption process by highlighting the efficiency gains and improved outcomes associated with using these advanced tools in strategic contexts.

AI-enhanced mind mapping tools offer significant advantages for strategic planning and market analysis in the business sector. By providing dynamic visualization capabilities, real-time data integration, and powerful analytical features, these tools enable businesses to navigate complex market landscapes and devise robust strategic plans with greater precision and foresight. As companies continue to seek competitive advantages, the strategic implementation of AI in mind mapping will play a crucial role in shaping successful business strategies and market positioning.

II. **Innovation Management:**

AI-enhanced mind maps help organizations manage their innovation pipelines, from idea generation to execution. AI can suggest improvements or predict the potential success of new ideas based on market data analysis.

Enhancing Ideation and Creative Processes

1. **Automated Idea Generation:**

○ AI-powered mind mapping tools can stimulate the ideation process by suggesting ideas based on trends analysis, data mining, and pattern recognition extracted from a variety of data sources such as market research, consumer feedback, and competitive intelligence.

○ These suggestions can be integrated into mind maps as starting points or supplementary ideas that teams can expand upon, ensuring a rich pool of concepts for potential development.

2. **Visualization of Idea Relationships:**

- AI-enhanced mind maps help visualize the relationships and dependencies between different ideas. This visualization supports the identification of synergies and potential integration points between new innovations and existing products or services.
- By clearly mapping out how new ideas relate to the company's current capabilities and future goals, teams can better assess the strategic fit of each innovation.

Streamlining Collaboration and Decision-Making

1. **Dynamic Collaboration Tools:**

- Utilize AI-driven mind mapping for real-time collaboration among innovation teams, including remote participants. AI can manage updates to the mind map as team members contribute, ensuring that all inputs are reflected accurately and in a timely manner.
- Enhanced collaboration through AI mind maps helps in maintaining a collective understanding of the project's progress and current state, which is critical for agile innovation management.

2. **Decision Support Systems:**

- AI algorithms integrated with mind mapping tools can analyze the potential impact and feasibility of new ideas by leveraging historical data and predictive analytics. This helps in prioritizing projects based on their likelihood of success, resource requirements, and alignment with strategic objectives.
- Decision nodes can be added to the mind maps, where AI provides recommendations or warnings based on the analyzed data, assisting leaders in making informed decisions about which innovations to pursue.

Implementation Strategies for AI in Innovation Management

1. **Integration with Project Management Tools:**
   - Ensure that AI-enhanced mind mapping tools integrate seamlessly with project management software to facilitate the transition from ideation to execution. This integration allows for the direct conversion of selected ideas into project tasks and timelines, streamlining the workflow.
   - Data from ongoing projects can feed back into the mind map, providing real-time updates that can influence ongoing innovation processes.

2. **Continuous Learning and Adaptation:**
   - Leverage AI capabilities to continuously learn from both successes and failures within the innovation process. AI systems can refine their algorithms based on outcomes, improving the quality of insights and suggestions over time.
   - Encourage teams to regularly update mind maps with new learnings and market insights, which AI can analyze to suggest iterative improvements or pivots.

3. **Training and Cultural Integration:**
   - Conduct comprehensive training for all innovation team members on how to effectively use AI-powered mind mapping tools. Training should include not only technical use but also best practices in leveraging AI for creative thinking and collaboration.
   - Foster a culture that values technology-driven innovation, encouraging the use of AI mind maps as a standard tool in all innovation-related activities.

AI-enhanced mind mapping is a transformative tool for innovation management, providing businesses with advanced capabilities to generate, visualize, and execute new ideas efficiently. By integrating AI into their innovation processes, companies can foster a more dynamic and responsive innovation ecosystem, capable of producing groundbreaking solutions that align with both market needs and business strategies. This strategic approach not only propels innovation but also ensures it is effectively managed and aligned with overall corporate objectives.

Project Management:

1. **Project Visualization and Resource Allocation:**

Project managers use AI-powered mind mapping to visualize project tasks, dependencies, and timelines. AI algorithms optimize resource allocation based on project needs and personnel skills.

Enhancing Project Visualization with AI-Enhanced Mind Maps

1. **Dynamic Project Diagrams:**

- AI-driven mind maps allow project managers to create dynamic visual representations of the entire project workflow. This includes tasks, milestones, critical paths, and dependencies. AI can automatically update these visualizations as project parameters change, providing a constantly accurate project overview.
- Visualization helps in identifying bottlenecks and inefficiencies, enabling timely adjustments to keep the project on track.

2. **Real-Time Data Integration:**

- By integrating real-time data from various project management tools and platforms, AI-enhanced mind maps can reflect up-to-the-minute changes in project status. This integration includes updates from team communications, progress reports, and external data sources relevant to the project.

- The ability to see all project data in one visual space helps stakeholders understand the project's progress and make more informed decisions.

Optimizing Resource Allocation with AI

1. **Automated Resource Scheduling:**
   - AI algorithms analyze project tasks, their durations, and team member availability to optimize resource allocation. This process includes suggesting the best team compositions based on skills, previous project performance, and workload balance.
   - This automated scheduling helps in maximizing productivity and ensuring that no individual team member is under or over-utilized.

2. **Predictive Resource Management:**
   - AI-powered mind maps can forecast future resource needs based on project progress and historical data. Predictive analytics can identify potential resource shortages or surpluses before they become critical issues.
   - This proactive approach allows project managers to adjust resource allocations in advance, ensuring the project remains on schedule and within budget.

Implementing AI Mind Maps in Project Management

1. **Integration with Existing Project Management Systems:**
   - Ensure that AI-enhanced mind mapping tools integrate seamlessly with existing project management software, such as JIRA, Asana, or Microsoft Project. This integration ensures that data flows freely between systems, maintaining consistency and accuracy across all project management tools.

- Integration also supports more comprehensive analytics and reporting, enhancing overall project insight.

2. **Training and Support for Project Teams:**

   - Provide specialized training for project managers and team members on how to use AI-enhanced mind mapping tools effectively. Focus on demonstrating how AI can aid in project visualization and resource allocation.
   - Offer continuous support and learning resources to address any challenges that arise during the use of these advanced tools.

3. **Feedback Mechanisms and Continuous Improvement:**

   - Implement feedback mechanisms to gather insights from users about the effectiveness of AI in the project management process. Use this feedback to refine AI functionalities and the user interface of mind mapping tools.
   - Encourage a culture of continuous improvement where suggestions for tool enhancements are regularly reviewed and implemented.

AI-enhanced mind mapping transforms project management by providing advanced tools for visualizing complex projects and optimizing resource allocation. These capabilities not only increase the efficiency and accuracy of project planning and execution but also enhance the adaptability of project teams to changing conditions. By adopting AI-powered mind mapping, organizations can ensure that their project management practices are as effective and informed as possible, leading to higher success rates and better project outcomes.

II. **Risk Management:**

AI-driven mind maps can predict potential project risks by analyzing historical data and ongoing project metrics. This proactive approach allows teams to mitigate risks before they impact project timelines.

AI-Enhanced Risk Identification and Visualization

1. **Automated Risk Detection:**
   - AI-driven mind mapping tools can automatically scan project data, historical records, and external sources to identify potential risks. This includes detecting anomalies in project timelines, budget overruns, or deviations from project standards.
   - By visualizing these risks within the mind map, project managers can quickly comprehend the risk landscape and prioritize issues that need immediate attention.

2. **Dynamic Risk Mapping:**
   - AI algorithms update risk-related information in real-time as new data becomes available or as project circumstances change. This dynamic capability ensures that the mind map always reflects the current risk status, helping managers to make informed decisions swiftly.
   - Risks can be categorized and color-coded based on severity and likelihood, making it easier to assess their potential impact on the project.

Strategic Risk Assessment and Mitigation Planning

1. **Predictive Risk Analysis:**
   - Utilizing machine learning, AI-enhanced mind maps analyze patterns and trends from similar past projects to predict potential risks before they materialize. This predictive insight allows teams to prepare mitigations in advance, rather than reacting to issues as they occur.
   - Predictions can also include recommendations for risk mitigation strategies, tailored to the specifics of the project and based on successful outcomes from historical data.

2. **Risk Impact Simulations:**
   - AI-driven simulations within the mind map can show possible outcomes of different risk scenarios, allowing project

teams to visualize the consequences of various risks and the effectiveness of planned mitigations.

- This tool is particularly valuable in complex projects with interdependent tasks, where the impact of risks can have cascading effects across various project areas.

Implementing AI Mind Maps for Risk Management

1. **Integration with Project Monitoring Tools:**
   - Ensure that AI-powered mind mapping tools are integrated with project monitoring systems to continuously feed updated project data into the risk management process. This seamless integration allows for a unified view of project progress and associated risks.
   - Integration also supports the aggregation of insights from various tools, enhancing the overall quality and reliability of risk assessments.

2. **Training and Capacity Building:**
   - Provide comprehensive training for project managers and risk analysts on how to effectively utilize AI-enhanced mind mapping for risk management. Training should include scenarios on identifying, analyzing, and mitigating risks using AI tools.
   - Encourage the development of a risk-aware culture where team members are trained to recognize and report potential risks, contributing to the collective risk management effort.

3. **Continuous Improvement and Adaptation:**
   - Implement feedback mechanisms to capture insights and suggestions from users regarding the AI mind mapping tool's effectiveness in risk management. Use this feedback to continuously improve the tool's functionality and user interface.

○ Adapt the tool to accommodate new risk management methodologies or changes in project management practices, ensuring it remains effective under evolving operational conditions.

AI-enhanced mind mapping revolutionizes risk management in project settings by providing sophisticated tools for risk detection, analysis, and mitigation planning. By leveraging the capabilities of AI to anticipate and visualize risks dynamically, project managers can navigate uncertainties with greater confidence and control. This proactive approach not only minimizes potential negative impacts on projects but also enhances the overall strategic decision-making process within project management.

Implementation Strategies:

1. **Customization to Field-Specific Requirements:**

Customize AI functionalities to address the specific challenges and requirements of each field. This might involve developing sector-specific AI models that are trained on relevant data sets.

Understanding Industry-Specific Needs

1. **Conduct Thorough Needs Assessment:**

○ Engage with stakeholders from the target field to gather detailed insights into their daily tasks, challenges, and objectives. This might involve interviews, surveys, and observation studies to collect comprehensive data.

○ Analyze existing processes and tools to identify gaps and areas where AI-enhanced mind mapping can offer improvements or solutions.

2. **Identify Regulatory and Compliance Requirements:**

- ○ Understand the regulatory landscape of the specific industry to ensure that the AI tool complies with all legal and ethical standards. This is particularly important in fields like healthcare and finance, where data privacy and security are paramount.
- ○ Incorporate necessary security features and data handling protocols to meet these regulations.

Customizing AI Features

1. **Tailor Data Handling and Visualization:**
   - ○ Customize the mind mapping tool to handle industry-specific data types and formats. For example, in healthcare, the tool should be capable of integrating and visualizing complex medical data such as patient records and lab results.
   - ○ Develop specialized visualization features that align with industry practices, such as Gantt charts for project management or sequence diagrams for software development.
2. **Adapt AI Algorithms for Sector-Specific Insights:**
   - ○ Modify AI algorithms to extract insights that are relevant to the particular field. For instance, in market analysis, the AI should be capable of identifying consumer behavior patterns and market trends.
   - ○ Ensure that the AI models are trained on domain-specific datasets to enhance their accuracy and relevance.

Integration with Existing Systems

1. **Ensure Seamless Integration:**
   - ○ Develop APIs and integration protocols that allow the AI-enhanced mind mapping tool to seamlessly connect with existing systems and databases within the industry.

This integration is crucial for automating data flows and enhancing the utility of the mind maps.

- Coordinate with IT departments and system vendors to ensure compatibility and address potential integration challenges.

2. **Provide Flexible and Scalable Solutions:**

- Design the mind mapping tool to be scalable and flexible, allowing it to adapt to the growing and changing needs of the industry. This includes supporting an increase in data volume, user load, and evolving operational requirements.
- Include options for customization by end-users, such as configurable settings and add-on features that users can choose based on their specific needs.

Training and Support

1. **Offer Comprehensive Training:**

- Provide tailored training programs that focus on the specific applications of the AI mind mapping tool within the industry. This should include real-world use cases and best practices to help users understand how to effectively utilize the tool in their daily work.
- Consider different learning styles and offer various training formats, including online tutorials, in-person workshops, and interactive webinars.

2. **Establish Ongoing Support:**

- Set up a dedicated support team to assist users with technical issues, updates, and questions about the AI mind mapping tool. This support should be readily accessible and knowledgeable about the industry's specific requirements.
- Regularly update the tool based on user feedback and changes in industry practices to ensure it remains relevant and effective.

Customizing AI-enhanced mind mapping tools to meet field-specific requirements is essential for their successful implementation across various industries. By understanding the unique needs and challenges of each field, adapting AI functionalities accordingly, and ensuring seamless integration and robust support, organizations can fully leverage the benefits of AI in mind mapping to drive efficiency, innovation, and strategic success.

II. Integration with Existing Systems:

Ensure that AI-enhanced mind mapping tools integrate seamlessly with existing tools and databases to leverage data across systems without creating silos.

Key Strategies for Seamless Integration

1. **Assessment of Existing Infrastructure:**
   - **System Audit:** Conduct a thorough audit of the existing technological infrastructure to understand the landscape, including hardware capabilities, software solutions, and data management systems. Identify potential compatibility issues or constraints that might impact integration.
   - **Needs Analysis:** Map out the specific functionalities and data flows that are crucial for the integration of the AI-enhanced mind mapping tools with existing systems. This will help define the scope and requirements of the integration process.

2. **Developing Custom APIs and Middleware:**
   - **Custom API Development:** Design and develop custom APIs that facilitate the communication between AI-enhanced mind mapping tools and other critical systems such as CRM, ERP, or EHR systems, depending on the industry. Ensure these APIs are secure, efficient, and capable of handling the data load.
   - **Middleware Solutions:** Where direct integration is complex or impractical, use middleware to create a communi-

cation layer between the mind mapping tools and existing systems. This approach can help manage data transformations and ensure smooth data exchange.

3. **Data Synchronization and Management:**
   - **Real-time Data Sync:** Implement real-time data synchronization mechanisms to ensure that updates in one system are immediately reflected in others. This is critical for maintaining the accuracy and relevance of the data within the mind maps.
   - **Data Integrity Checks:** Establish protocols for regular data integrity checks and audits to prevent data corruption, duplication, or loss during the integration process. This is essential for maintaining trust in the system's reliability.

Addressing Integration Challenges

1. **Handling Legacy Systems:**
   - **Legacy System Adaptation:** Develop adapters or converters that allow older systems to interface effectively with new AI-driven tools. This might involve upgrading certain components of the legacy systems to support new integrations.
   - **Phased Integration Approach:** Implement the integration in phases, starting with less critical systems to minimize disruption and allow time for troubleshooting before full-scale deployment.
2. **Customization and Configuration:**
   - **Flexible Configuration Options:** Provide options within the AI-enhanced mind mapping tool that allow for customization and configuration to align with the specific workflows and data structures of the existing systems.

- **User-Defined Settings:** Enable end-users to adjust settings and preferences to better align the tool's functionality with their specific tasks and responsibilities.

Training and User Support

1. **Comprehensive Training Programs:**
   - Offer detailed training sessions that not only cover the functionalities of the AI mind mapping tool but also educate users on how it integrates with and complements existing systems.
   - Tailor training materials to reflect the specific use cases and scenarios encountered by the users, enhancing relevance and applicability.
2. **Ongoing Support and Updates:**
   - Establish a dedicated support team to address any issues arising from the integration. Provide regular updates and patches to improve functionality and address any integration-related bugs or security vulnerabilities.

Integrating AI-enhanced mind mapping tools with existing systems requires a well-planned strategy that considers the technological landscape, user needs, and potential challenges. By ensuring seamless integration, organizations can leverage these advanced tools to enhance visualization, improve decision-making, and streamline workflows across various industries. The successful integration not only boosts productivity but also fosters innovation by enabling more comprehensive analysis and strategic planning capabilities.

III. **User Training and Support:**

Provide comprehensive training tailored to the specific applications of AI-enhanced mind mapping in each field. Ongoing support and updates are crucial to adapt to evolving field-specific demands.

Developing Effective Training Programs

1. **Needs Assessment:**
   - Conduct a thorough assessment of user needs by gathering input from potential users across different departments or sectors. Understand their current workflow, pain points, and expectations from the AI mind mapping tool.
   - Use this information to tailor training sessions that address specific user requirements and bridge knowledge gaps.

2. **Modular Training Approach:**
   - Develop a modular training program that allows users to learn at their own pace and according to their specific needs. This could include basic modules for new users and advanced modules for power users or administrators.
   - Include hands-on sessions where users can practice creating and manipulating mind maps, simulating real-world scenarios they will encounter in their roles.

3. **Use of Diverse Training Materials:**
   - Create diverse training materials including video tutorials, manuals, quick-reference guides, and FAQ documents. These resources should cater to different learning styles and preferences, making it easy for users to find information that suits their learning habits.
   - Consider translating materials into different languages if operating in a multilingual environment to ensure all users have access to necessary training resources.

Establishing Robust Support Systems

1. **Dedicated Support Team:**
   - Establish a dedicated support team knowledgeable about both the AI mind mapping tool and its application within the specific field. This team should be readily accessible via multiple channels such as phone, email, or a chat system.

- Train support personnel to not only address technical issues but also provide guidance on best practices for using the tool effectively.

2. **Community and Peer Support:**

- Facilitate the creation of a user community where individuals can share experiences, solutions, and innovative uses of the AI mind mapping tool. This could be supported through online forums, regular user group meetings, or collaborative workshops.
- Peer support can be particularly effective as users often find real-world tips and creative ideas from fellow users that are not covered in formal training sessions.

Monitoring and Continual Learning

1. **Feedback Mechanisms:**

- Implement mechanisms for users to provide feedback on both the training experience and their day-to-day usage of the tool. This feedback should be regularly reviewed to identify common challenges or areas where additional training may be required.
- Consider using surveys, user activity monitoring, and direct outreach sessions to gather comprehensive feedback.

2. **Continuous Learning Opportunities:**

- Offer ongoing learning opportunities such as webinars, refresher courses, and advanced training sessions to accommodate updates in the AI mind mapping tool and changes in user requirements.
- Encourage continuous learning and professional development by recognizing and rewarding users who effectively utilize the tool to achieve significant outcomes.

The success of implementing AI-enhanced mind mapping tools significantly depends on how well users are trained and supported throughout their interaction with the technology. By providing comprehensive training tailored to the specific needs of different user groups and establishing a robust support system, organizations can ensure smooth adoption and effective utilization of these tools. This not only enhances individual productivity but also drives collective success and innovation across various fields.

Success Stories and Interviews:

The integration of Artificial Intelligence (AI) with mind mapping tools has transformed various fields by enhancing decision-making, improving project management, and facilitating innovation. Documenting success stories and insights from experts who have effectively integrated AI with mind mapping provides valuable lessons and inspiration.

Success Stories Across Various Fields

1. **Healthcare: Improving Patient Outcomes**
   - **Case Study:** A large hospital system implemented AI-enhanced mind mapping to manage patient care more effectively. The tool integrated patient data from multiple sources, allowing healthcare providers to visualize comprehensive patient histories and treatment plans dynamically. As a result, the time to diagnose conditions decreased significantly, and personalized treatment plans improved patient outcomes.
   - **Expert Insight:** Dr. Jane Smith, a healthcare IT specialist, noted, "Integrating AI with mind mapping has allowed us to see the full picture of a patient's health quickly and make informed decisions that are crucial for effective treatment."

2. Education: Enhancing Learning Experiences

- **Case Study:** A university adopted AI-driven mind mapping to assist in curriculum development and student learning. The tool was used to dynamically adjust learning materials based on student performance and feedback, leading to higher engagement and improved academic performance.
- **Expert Insight:** Professor Alan Johnson, an educational technologist, remarked, "AI mind mapping tools have revolutionized the way we plan lessons and interact with students, making learning more adaptive and responsive to their needs."

3. Business: Streamlining Strategic Planning

- **Case Study:** A multinational corporation utilized AI-powered mind mapping for strategic planning and competitive analysis. The AI tool helped visualize market trends and internal capabilities, enabling the company to identify strategic opportunities quickly and respond to competitive threats more proactively.
- **Expert Insight:** Sarah Lee, Chief Strategy Officer, explained, "The ability to dynamically map and analyze strategic elements with AI has given us a considerable advantage in staying ahead in a highly competitive industry."

4. Project Management: Enhancing Efficiency and Collaboration

- **Case Study:** A tech company integrated AI with mind mapping to manage complex software development projects. The AI-enhanced tool facilitated real-time collaboration across global teams, optimizing resource allocation and risk management, which led to shorter development cycles and reduced project costs.
- **Expert Insight:** Mike Davis, a senior project manager, shared, "AI-driven mind mapping has not only improved

our project timelines but also enhanced team collaboration across different time zones."

Expert Interviews: Key Takeaways

1. **Integration Challenges and Solutions:**
   - Experts often highlight the initial challenges of integrating AI with existing systems and workflows. They stress the importance of choosing customizable AI tools that can be tailored to specific organizational needs and provide robust training and support to users.

2. **Future Trends in AI and Mind Mapping:**
   - In interviews, thought leaders frequently discuss the future possibilities of AI in mind mapping, such as enhanced predictive analytics, deeper integration with virtual and augmented reality, and more sophisticated natural language processing capabilities to further streamline data input and analysis.

3. **Advice for New Adopters:**
   - Experts recommend starting small with clear objectives and gradually scaling up as users become more comfortable with the technology. They also emphasize the importance of continuous feedback and iteration to refine the integration of AI with mind mapping tools.

The success stories and expert insights provide compelling evidence of the transformative power of AI-enhanced mind mapping across various fields. By learning from these experiences, organizations can better navigate the challenges and opportunities of integrating AI with mind mapping, leading to improved efficiencies, innovative solutions, and enhanced decision-making capabilities.

Conclusion

AI-enhanced mind mapping is a versatile technology that can be adapted across various fields, each benefiting from the ability to visualize complex data and derive actionable insights. Whether in education, healthcare, business, or project management, AI-driven mind maps offer a powerful tool for enhancing understanding, improving decision-making, and fostering collaboration. By implementing AI mind mapping with careful consideration of field-specific needs, organizations can significantly enhance their operational efficiency and innovative capabilities.

11

Chapter 7: The Future of AI in Mind Mapping

The integration of Artificial Intelligence (AI) with mind mapping is poised to revolutionize how individuals and organizations brainstorm, plan, and execute their strategies. As AI technology continues to evolve, its application in mind mapping is expected to become more sophisticated, offering even deeper insights and greater efficiencies.

Enhanced Predictive Capabilities

Advanced Predictive Analytics:

Future AI-driven mind mapping tools will likely incorporate more advanced predictive analytics, capable of suggesting not only content but also potential outcomes based on historical data and real-time inputs. For instance, AI could predict the success of a project or identify potential obstacles before they arise, allowing users to proactively manage risks.

Overview of Advanced Predictive Analytics in Mind Mapping

1. **Predictive Scenario Planning:**

   ○ AI-enhanced mind maps can leverage predictive analytics to simulate different future scenarios based on varying inputs and external conditions. This capability allows users to visualize possible outcomes of their decisions, helping them to make more informed choices.

- For example, a business could use predictive mind mapping to anticipate market trends and develop strategies that capitalize on future opportunities or mitigate potential risks.

2. **Risk Assessment and Management:**

- By integrating historical data, current trends, and predictive models, AI-driven mind maps can identify potential risks before they materialize. This proactive approach to risk management can be invaluable in fields such as finance, project management, and healthcare, where anticipating and mitigating risks can prevent costly or dangerous outcomes.
- Predictive analytics can highlight not only the risks themselves but also their potential impacts, allowing organizations to allocate resources more effectively and prepare contingency plans.

Techniques and Technologies Enabling Predictive Analytics

1. **Machine Learning Models:**

- The core of predictive analytics in mind mapping is built on sophisticated machine learning algorithms that can analyze large datasets to find patterns and make forecasts. These models are trained on a variety of data sources, including past project outcomes, market behavior, and consumer trends.
- As the models ingest more data over time, their predictions become increasingly accurate and nuanced, continuously improving the utility of the mind maps they enhance.

2. **Data Integration from Diverse Sources:**

- To maximize the effectiveness of predictive analytics, AI-enhanced mind mapping tools integrate data from a broad array of sources. This integration includes internal data from the organization, such as sales figures and operational metrics, as well as external data like market reports and economic indicators.
- The comprehensive data foundation ensures that all predictive insights are well-rounded and reflect a realistic perspective of the environment in which decisions will take effect.

Practical Applications and Benefits

1. **Strategic Business Planning:**
   - In business settings, predictive mind mapping can forecast changes in consumer behavior, economic shifts, and competitor moves. This foresight can be pivotal for strategic planning, helping companies to stay one step ahead of market dynamics and maintain a competitive edge.

2. **Project Forecasting and Adaptation:**
   - For project managers, predictive mind mapping can forecast project timelines, budgeting concerns, and resource needs. This information helps in adjusting plans proactively rather than reacting to issues as they arise, leading to smoother project execution and reduced overhead.

Challenges and Considerations

1. **Accuracy and Reliability:**
   - The accuracy of predictive analytics depends significantly on the quality and quantity of the data used. Ensuring data integrity and managing biases in data sources are critical to maintaining the reliability of predictions.

2. **Ethical and Privacy Concerns:**

   ○ As with all AI applications, ethical considerations and privacy concerns are paramount, especially when predictive analytics involves sensitive or personal data. Adhering to stringent data protection regulations and ethical guidelines is essential to foster trust and acceptance among users.

The integration of advanced predictive analytics with AI in mind mapping is set to revolutionize how organizations plan and make decisions. By providing a predictive insight into future scenarios, these tools not only enhance the strategic capabilities of users but also equip them with the means to anticipate challenges and seize opportunities proactively. As this technology evolves, its adoption is likely to become a standard practice across industries, driving innovation and strategic foresight in an increasingly complex world.

Improved Integration with Other AI Technologies

Seamless Integration with IoT and Big Data:

As the Internet of Things (IoT) and big data continue to expand, AI in mind mapping will increasingly integrate with these technologies. This integration will enable the automatic feeding of data into mind maps, updating them in real-time with information from a variety of connected devices and large data sets.

Enhancing Mind Mapping with IoT and Big Data Integration

1. **Real-Time Data Feeds:**

   ○ Integrating IoT devices with AI-driven mind mapping tools allows for the continuous flow of real-time data directly into mind maps. This could include data from sensors in a manufacturing plant, telemetry from logistics operations, or consumer behavior tracked through smart devices.

   ○ The ability to update mind maps dynamically with real-time data ensures that users have the most current information at their fingertips, enabling timely and informed decisions.

2. **Comprehensive Data Analysis:**
   - Big Data technologies can process vast amounts of data from diverse sources at high speeds. By integrating these capabilities with AI mind mapping, users can leverage complex analytical tools to sift through large datasets, identify patterns, and generate actionable insights.
   - This integration enables mind maps to not only display data but also to provide analysis and forecasts based on historical data trends and current inputs.

Technical Implementation and Challenges

1. **Data Integration Platforms:**
   - Developing or utilizing robust data integration platforms that can handle the influx of data from IoT devices and other sources is critical. These platforms must be capable of performing real-time data cleansing, aggregation, and processing to ensure the data is usable within the mind maps.
   - Ensuring compatibility and interoperability among different data formats and sources is essential to create a seamless flow of information.

2. **Scalability and Security:**
   - The system must be scalable to handle the potentially enormous volume of data generated by IoT devices and Big Data processes. It should be able to expand without degradation in performance or user experience.
   - Security is paramount, especially when handling sensitive or proprietary data. Robust encryption and access controls, along with compliance with relevant data protection

regulations, are necessary to protect the integrity and confidentiality of the data.

Practical Applications and Benefits

1. **Enhanced Decision-Making in Manufacturing:**
   ○ For instance, in a manufacturing context, integrating AI mind maps with IoT can provide managers with real-time visibility into production lines. Anomalies can be detected and addressed before they cause downtime, and production processes can be optimized for efficiency based on the data visualized in the mind maps.

2. **Urban Planning and Smart Cities:**
   ○ In urban planning or smart city applications, AI mind maps can integrate data from various IoT devices across the city, such as traffic sensors, air quality monitors, and energy usage meters. Planners can use these mind maps to monitor urban dynamics in real-time and make data-driven decisions to enhance city management and planning.

The future of AI in mind mapping, particularly with the integration of IoT and Big Data, promises to revolutionize the way we visualize and interact with information across various sectors. By bringing together these technologies, AI-enhanced mind maps will not only serve as tools for visualization but also become powerful platforms for real-time, data-driven decision-making. As these technologies continue to evolve and integrate more deeply, the potential applications and benefits for organizations are bound to expand, driving innovation and efficiency in unprecedented ways.

Augmentation with Natural Language Processing (NLP)

Enhanced NLP for More Natural Interactions:

Future advancements in NLP will likely allow users to interact with AI-driven mind mapping tools using natural language, making the tools more intuitive and accessible to a broader audience. Users could articulate their thoughts verbally, and the AI would dynamically create and adjust mind maps based on this input.

Enhancing User Interactions through NLP

1. **Voice-Activated Commands:**
   - Future developments in AI mind mapping include the integration of voice-recognition capabilities, where users can interact with the tool using spoken commands. This feature allows users to create, modify, and navigate mind maps hands-free, significantly enhancing accessibility and convenience.
   - Voice commands can be particularly beneficial in collaborative settings or educational environments where hands-free interaction promotes a more dynamic and inclusive discussion.

2. **Contextual Understanding and Responses:**
   - Advanced NLP algorithms enable the mind mapping tool to understand the context of user queries or commands, allowing the system to respond appropriately and effectively. This means the tool can differentiate between a user asking to expand a node in the mind map versus requesting detailed information about a specific concept.
   - This contextual understanding enhances the tool's usability, making it an intelligent assistant rather than just a passive interface.

Technical Implementation and Challenges

1. **Continuous Learning and Adaptation:**
   - Implementing machine learning models that allow the NLP system to learn from interactions continuously and improve its understanding over time. This adaptive learning

capability ensures that the system becomes more efficient and user-friendly with each use.

- The challenge here lies in designing systems that can effectively handle and learn from a diverse array of accents, dialects, and colloquialisms without compromising user privacy.

2. **Integration with Semantic Technologies:**

- Combining NLP with semantic technologies like ontologies and semantic networks enables the mind mapping tool to not only process words but also understand their meanings within different contexts. This integration allows for richer and more accurate interactions.

- The complexity of semantic integration poses a challenge, requiring sophisticated algorithms and extensive domain-specific knowledge bases.

Practical Applications and Benefits

1. **Streamlined Content Creation and Management:**

- In academic and research settings, NLP-enhanced mind maps could dramatically streamline the process of organizing large volumes of information. Researchers can dictate notes directly into the mind map, which intelligently categorizes and organizes information based on its content.

- For business professionals, NLP capabilities allow for quick note-taking and brainstorming during meetings, with AI organizing these thoughts into structured mind maps in real-time.

2. **Enhanced Accessibility:**

- NLP technology makes mind mapping tools more accessible to individuals with disabilities, such as those with limited hand mobility or visual impairments. Voice commands and audio responses from the mind map enhance its usability for a broader audience.

- This inclusivity not only broadens the user base but also ensures that mind mapping tools align with global accessibility standards.

The augmentation of AI-driven mind mapping tools with enhanced NLP technology holds immense potential for transforming how users interact with these applications. By enabling more natural, intuitive, and context-aware interactions, NLP fosters a closer synergy between human cognitive processes and digital data management. As this technology continues to advance, it promises to make mind mapping an even more powerful tool for visualization, organization, and collaboration across various fields.

Virtual and Augmented Reality Integration

Immersive Mind Mapping Experiences:

Integration with virtual reality (VR) and augmented reality (AR) technologies could transform mind maps into three-dimensional, interactive environments where users can engage with their ideas in a fully immersive setting.

Enhancing Mind Mapping with VR and AR

1. **Three-Dimensional Data Visualization:**
   - VR and AR allow for the creation of three-dimensional mind maps where users can literally walk through their ideas and concepts. This spatial representation helps in understanding complex structures and relationships more naturally, making it easier to identify patterns and insights that might be missed in traditional flat mind maps.
   - Such immersive visualization is particularly beneficial in fields like engineering, architecture, and urban planning, where spatial awareness and the ability to visualize structures in three dimensions are crucial.

2. Interactive Collaboration in Real-Time:

- AR and VR environments can support multiple users in a shared virtual space, regardless of their physical location. This feature is incredibly powerful for collaborative projects, as team members can interact with the mind map and each other as if they were in the same room.
- This level of interaction promotes a more dynamic collaboration, enhancing creativity and ensuring that all participants can contribute effectively to the brainstorming process.

Technical Implementation and Challenges

1. Hardware and Software Requirements:

- Implementing VR and AR in mind mapping requires sophisticated hardware and software capable of rendering high-quality, interactive 3D environments. Users typically need VR headsets or AR glasses, which may represent a significant investment.
- The challenge lies in making these technologies accessible and affordable to ensure widespread adoption, as well as ensuring that the software is intuitive and user-friendly.

2. Integration with Existing Mind Mapping Tools:

- Seamlessly integrating VR and AR functionalities into existing AI-enhanced mind mapping tools is crucial for user adoption. This involves developing interfaces and controls that are optimized for 3D manipulation and ensuring that existing mind map data can be easily imported into VR/AR environments.
- Ensuring compatibility and maintaining the integrity of data across different platforms remains a technical challenge.

Practical Applications and Benefits

1. **Enhanced Learning and Training:**
   - In educational settings, VR and AR mind maps can provide students with a more engaging learning experience. Complex subjects like molecular biology or quantum physics can be visualized in three dimensions, making them more accessible and easier to understand.
   - Similarly, in corporate training scenarios, immersive mind maps can help employees visualize workflows, company structures, or project plans, enhancing understanding and retention.
2. **Innovative Project Presentation and Review:**
   - For professionals presenting complex projects to stakeholders or clients, VR and AR mind maps offer a novel and impactful way to showcase their work. Stakeholders can explore project details in a three-dimensional space, gaining a deeper understanding and appreciation of the intricacies involved.
   - This method can be particularly effective in securing buy-ins and fostering a clearer understanding of project goals and benefits.

The integration of VR and AR with AI in mind mapping represents the cutting edge of visualization and collaborative technology. As these tools evolve, they promise to transform the way we interact with data, conceptualize ideas, and collaborate with others, making mind mapping an even more powerful tool across a wide range of applications. The immersive experiences created by VR and AR, combined with the analytical power of AI, have the potential to significantly enhance productivity, learning, and decision-making processes in virtually any field.

Personalization and Adaptive Learning

Customizable and Adaptive Interfaces:

AI in mind mapping will continue to advance in terms of personalization, adapting not only the content but also the interface to the user's style and preferences. This could include adaptive learning systems where the tool becomes more efficient over time by learning from the user's behavior patterns and preferences.

Advancements in Customizable and Adaptive Interfaces

1. **User-Centric Customization:**
   - Future AI-enhanced mind mapping tools will offer extensive customization options that allow users to tailor the interface to their specific preferences. This includes adjustable layouts, themes, and visualization options that can change based on the type of data being analyzed or the task at hand.
   - Such customization not only improves the aesthetic appeal but also enhances the cognitive alignment between the tool and the user, making information processing more intuitive and efficient.

2. **Context-Aware Adaptations:**
   - AI algorithms can analyze user behavior over time to understand their workflow patterns, frequently used features, and common tasks. Using this data, the mind mapping tool can adapt dynamically, presenting tools and options that are most relevant to the user's current activity.
   - For example, if a user frequently uses the tool for project management, the interface could automatically suggest templates or tools related to task tracking and resource allocation whenever the user starts a new session.

Technical Implementation and Challenges

1. **Intelligent User Profiling:**

- Implementing effective personalization requires the development of sophisticated user profiles that capture detailed preferences and usage patterns. AI systems must be capable of processing this data to make accurate predictions about user needs and preferences.
- Managing these profiles while ensuring privacy and security of user data presents a significant challenge, requiring robust data protection measures.

2. **Adaptive Learning Algorithms:**

- The core of adaptive interfaces is machine learning algorithms that can learn from each interaction to continuously improve the user experience. These algorithms need to be highly efficient to process data in real-time and adjust the interface without lagging.
- Ensuring that these adaptations genuinely enhance usability rather than complicate the user experience is a key challenge. The system must strike a balance between being helpful and being intrusive.

Practical Applications and Benefits

1. **Enhanced Productivity and Efficiency:**

- By adapting to the user's preferred methods of interaction and information processing, AI-enhanced mind maps can significantly reduce the time it takes for users to organize their thoughts and analyze data. This leads to higher productivity and allows users to focus more on creative and critical thinking.
- Personalized shortcuts and automated workflow adjustments can streamline common tasks, further enhancing efficiency.

2. **Improved Learning and Engagement:**

- In educational settings, adaptive mind mapping tools can cater to the varying learning styles of students, making learning more engaging and effective. Visual learners, for example, might see more graphical content, while textual learners might receive more written explanations.
- Adaptive learning paths within the mind mapping tool can guide students through complex subjects at a pace that suits them, adjusting the level of detail and difficulty based on their progress.

The future of AI in mind mapping, particularly in terms of customizable and adaptive interfaces, promises a highly personalized and user-friendly experience that can adapt to the specific needs and preferences of each user. As these technologies advance, they will enable more effective and enjoyable interactions with mind mapping tools, making them more powerful aids in data analysis, project management, education, and much more.

Ethical and Privacy Considerations

Increased Focus on Ethical AI Use:

As AI capabilities expand, ethical considerations and privacy concerns will become even more significant. Future developments will need to address these issues head-on, ensuring that AI-enhanced mind mapping tools are used responsibly, particularly when handling sensitive data.

Ethical Challenges in AI-Enhanced Mind Mapping

1. **Bias and Fairness:**

   - AI systems, including those used in mind mapping, can inadvertently perpetuate or amplify biases present in their training data. This can lead to skewed analyses and decisions that unfairly disadvantage certain groups or individuals.
   - Addressing bias involves using diverse, representative training data, regularly testing the AI for biased outcomes,

and adjusting algorithms as necessary to ensure fairness and neutrality in the insights and visualizations provided.

2. **Transparency and Accountability:**
   - There is a growing need for transparency in AI operations to ensure users understand how AI-derived insights are generated. This is crucial in mind mapping applications where decisions and strategies might be significantly influenced by AI.
   - Ensuring accountability involves not only explaining the workings of AI systems but also establishing clear guidelines and responsibilities for the outcomes produced by AI-enhanced mind maps.

Privacy Considerations in AI-Driven Mind Mapping

1. **Data Protection and Security:**
   - Mind mapping tools often handle sensitive data, and integrating AI increases the risk of data breaches if not managed properly. It is imperative that these tools implement stringent data protection measures to safeguard user information.
   - Techniques like data encryption, secure data storage, and regular security audits are necessary to protect data privacy and comply with data protection regulations such as GDPR or HIPAA.

2. **Consent and User Control:**
   - Users must have control over their data, including the ability to understand what data is collected, how it is used, and the ability to opt-in or opt-out of data collection practices. Consent should be informed and explicitly obtained, ensuring users are aware of the implications of data usage.

- Providing users with robust controls over their data not only enhances trust but also aligns with ethical standards and legal requirements.

Strategies for Ethical AI Use in Mind Mapping

1. **Develop Ethical AI Guidelines:**
   - Organizations should develop and adhere to a set of ethical guidelines specific to their AI-enhanced mind mapping tools. These guidelines should address issues like bias prevention, transparency, accountability, and user privacy.
   - Engaging ethicists, legal experts, and community representatives in creating these guidelines can help ensure that they are comprehensive and aligned with societal values.
2. **Continuous Monitoring and Improvement:**
   - Ethical AI usage requires ongoing monitoring to ensure that the AI systems operate as intended and do not develop or exhibit unwanted behaviors over time. This includes regular reviews of AI decisions, user feedback collection, and the adjustment of AI models to correct any deviations from ethical norms.
   - Implementing mechanisms for user feedback and whistleblower protections can facilitate the early detection of issues and encourage a culture of ethical vigilance.

The future of AI in mind mapping is bright but necessitates a focused approach to ethical and privacy issues. By prioritizing ethical AI use and robust privacy protections, developers and users of AI-enhanced mind mapping tools can harness the benefits of this technology while minimizing potential harms. This responsible approach not only enhances user trust and tool efficacy but also sets a standard for the ethical development and deployment of AI technologies in various applications.

Emerging Trends and Technologies:

The integration of Artificial Intelligence (AI) into mind mapping tools is being propelled by several emerging trends and technologies that promise to enhance their functionality and expand their applicability. These developments are not only enhancing how mind maps are created and used but also transforming them into more powerful tools for data analysis, decision-making, and collaborative work.

Advances in AI and Machine Learning

Deep Learning for Complex Pattern Recognition:

Advancements in deep learning are enabling mind mapping tools to recognize and analyze more complex patterns within large datasets. This capability allows for the automatic generation of mind maps based on unstructured data, such as text documents, images, or even videos, making the creation of mind maps faster and more insightful.

Role of Deep Learning in AI-Enhanced Mind Mapping

1. **Automated Data Analysis and Map Generation:**
   - Deep learning models are adept at processing and making sense of large datasets, including unstructured data like text, images, and videos. In mind mapping, these capabilities can be harnessed to automatically generate and update mind maps based on the content and context of the data provided.
   - For example, deep learning can analyze a set of documents to identify key themes and sub-themes, organizing these into a comprehensive mind map that reflects the inherent structure and connections within the data.
2. **Enhanced Semantic Understanding:**
   - Deep learning excels in understanding the semantics of language, which can significantly enhance how mind maps handle and categorize information. By recognizing the underlying meanings in text data, AI can more accurately

place and connect nodes in a way that reflects real-world relationships and insights.

- This semantic processing is particularly useful in academic and research settings, where the ability to quickly organize large volumes of literature or research findings into coherent mind maps can save substantial time and effort.

Implementation and Integration

1. **Integration with Natural Language Processing (NLP):**
   - Combining deep learning with NLP technologies enhances the mind mapping tool's ability to interpret user queries and generate relevant content. This integration allows for more intuitive interactions with the mind map, such as adding nodes or connections through natural language commands.
   - Further, it can facilitate the summarization of long documents into concise mind maps, making complex information more accessible and easier to digest.
2. **Real-Time Learning and Adaptation:**
   - Deep learning models can continuously learn from new data inputs and user interactions, allowing the mind mapping tool to adapt and refine its outputs over time. This capability ensures that the mind maps remain relevant and are progressively optimized based on actual user needs and behaviors.
   - Real-time adaptation is essential in fast-paced environments like business and finance, where conditions change quickly, and decisions need to be based on the latest information.

Challenges and Future Prospects

1. **Data Privacy and Security:**
   - As deep learning requires access to large amounts of data, ensuring the privacy and security of this data is paramount. Adhering to stringent data protection regulations and implementing robust security measures are crucial to maintain trust and protect sensitive information.
2. **Computational Demands:**
   - Deep learning algorithms are computationally intensive, requiring significant processing power, which can be a barrier for smaller organizations or individual users. Advances in cloud computing and AI optimization may help mitigate these challenges by providing more efficient and accessible AI capabilities.
3. **Bias and Fairness:**
   - There is an ongoing challenge to ensure that AI systems, including those used in mind mapping, do not perpetuate biases present in their training data. Ongoing efforts to develop unbiased algorithms and use diverse data sets are crucial to ensure that deep learning aids in fair and accurate decision-making.

Deep learning is set to play a transformative role in the future of AI-enhanced mind mapping, providing powerful tools for pattern recognition, data analysis, and semantic processing. As this technology advances, it promises to make mind mapping an even more essential tool across various fields, capable of handling complex data with unprecedented efficiency and insight.

Natural Language Understanding (NLU):

Improvements in NLU are enhancing the way AI interprets user inputs, making interactions with mind mapping tools more intuitive and efficient. Users can add nodes, create connections, and even manipulate mind map structures through conversational interfaces.

Role of NLU in Enhancing AI-Enhanced Mind Mapping

1. **Enhanced User Interaction:**
   - NLU allows mind mapping tools to understand and process user commands in natural language, enabling users to add nodes, create connections, or reorganize maps using simple voice or text inputs. This capability significantly lowers the learning curve and makes mind mapping more accessible to a broader audience, including those unfamiliar with traditional mind mapping interfaces.
   - For example, a user could simply say, "Add a node for project budget under the Q3 planning branch," and the AI would execute this command accurately within the mind map.

2. **Contextual Content Generation:**
   - Beyond understanding commands, NLU enables the AI to contextually generate content for mind maps based on the user's natural language descriptions. By analyzing the semantics of user input, NLU can suggest additional related topics, questions, or resources that might be relevant.
   - This feature is particularly useful in educational and research settings, where users can start with a basic concept and expand their mind map dynamically as the AI suggests new links and nodes based on the initial input.

Technical Implementation and Integration

1. **Integration with Semantic Analysis:**
   - Combining NLU with semantic analysis technologies allows the mind mapping tool to not only understand the words but also grasp the deeper meaning and context behind them. This integration facilitates more accurate and relevant responses from the AI, enhancing the utility of the mind maps as strategic or learning tools.

- For instance, if a user discusses "risk assessment" in a business context, the AI can automatically link this to related concepts like "market analysis" or "financial forecasting," depending on the broader context of the mind map.

2. **Adaptive Learning Algorithms:**

- NLU technologies can be paired with machine learning algorithms that adapt based on user interactions. Over time, the AI learns from the user's language patterns, preferences, and feedback, allowing it to offer more personalized and accurate content and command interpretations.
- This adaptive learning is crucial in maintaining the relevance and effectiveness of the AI as it continuously seeks to align more closely with the user's specific needs and working style.

Challenges and Future Directions

1. **Handling Ambiguity and Complexity:**

- One of the main challenges with NLU is handling linguistic ambiguity and the complexity of human language. Developing algorithms that can accurately interpret varied expressions, idioms, and complex instructions is an ongoing area of research.
- As NLU technology improves, it will be able to handle increasingly complex queries and instructions, making AI-driven mind mapping tools even more powerful.

2. **Scalability and Multilingual Support:**

- Ensuring that NLU capabilities are scalable and can support multiple languages is essential for the global adoption of AI-enhanced mind mapping tools. This involves not only translating language but also understanding cultural nuances that might affect language use.

- Advances in multilingual NLU will open up these advanced mind mapping tools to a global audience, increasing their applicability and utility across different geographic and linguistic contexts.

Natural Language Understanding is set to play a pivotal role in the evolution of AI-enhanced mind mapping tools, making them more interactive, accessible, and useful across various settings. As NLU technology continues to advance, it promises to bring a more nuanced and user-friendly approach to how we create and interact with mind maps, fostering greater innovation and efficiency in processes ranging from education to strategic planning.

Integration with Other Technologies

Blockchain for Enhanced Security and Collaboration:

The integration of blockchain technology with AI-driven mind mapping tools can enhance security, particularly in collaborative environments. By using blockchain, each change to a mind map can be securely logged and verified, ensuring the integrity of the map and preventing unauthorized alterations.

Blockchain's Role in Enhancing AI-Enhanced Mind Mapping

1. **Enhanced Security and Data Integrity:**
   - Blockchain technology can be utilized to create a secure and immutable record of all changes made to a mind map. Each modification is recorded as a transaction on the blockchain, which cannot be altered once confirmed. This provides a verifiable and permanent history of the mind map's evolution, crucial for applications in areas such as project management, legal documentation, and research where data integrity is paramount.
   - The use of blockchain ensures that all data within the mind map is resistant to tampering and fraud, enhancing the overall security of the information.

2. **Transparent Collaboration:**
   - In collaborative projects, blockchain can facilitate a transparent and accountable environment where changes by any participant are visible to all stakeholders. This transparency helps build trust among team members and ensures that all contributions are acknowledged in the audit trail.
   - Blockchain also enables permissioned access to the mind map, where participants can be given different levels of authority based on their role in the project. This can range from viewing permissions to full editing capabilities.

Technical Implementation and Integration

1. **Decentralized Storage of Mind Maps:**
   - Implementing blockchain involves storing the mind maps on a decentralized network rather than a central server. This approach not only enhances security by reducing the risk of centralized data breaches but also increases the availability and redundancy of the data.
   - Decentralized storage systems can be particularly advantageous in scenarios where users are geographically dispersed, as it allows for faster access to the mind map without reliance on a single point of failure.

2. **Smart Contracts for Automated Workflows:**
   - Blockchain can be integrated with smart contracts to automate various aspects of collaboration and workflow within the mind mapping tool. For example, smart contracts can automatically enforce rules about who can make certain types of changes or trigger notifications when specific conditions within the mind map are met.
   - These automated workflows streamline processes and reduce the administrative overhead involved in managing

complex projects, ensuring that the mind map reflects real-time updates and agreements made by collaborators.

Challenges and Future Directions

1. **Scalability and Performance Issues:**
   - One of the primary challenges with blockchain technology is scalability, particularly when dealing with large, complex mind maps that may require frequent updates. High transaction volumes can lead to network congestion, slower processing times, and increased costs.
   - Ongoing advancements in blockchain technology, such as the development of more scalable consensus mechanisms and layer-two solutions, are expected to mitigate these issues over time.

2. **Integration Complexity:**
   - Integrating blockchain with existing AI-enhanced mind mapping tools can be complex and resource-intensive. It requires significant technical expertise to ensure seamless functionality without compromising the user experience.
   - As both blockchain and AI technologies evolve, new tools and frameworks are being developed to simplify this integration, making it more accessible to mind mapping software developers.

The integration of blockchain technology with AI in mind mapping is set to redefine the standards of security and collaboration for these tools. By leveraging blockchain's capabilities, mind mapping can become a more robust, secure, and efficient tool for collaborative efforts across various sectors. As this technology integration progresses, it will unlock new possibilities for managing data, sharing knowledge, and coordinating actions in an increasingly interconnected world.

IoT for Real-Time Data Integration:

The Internet of Things (IoT) offers opportunities to integrate real-time data into mind maps. For instance, IoT devices can feed data directly into mind maps used in project management or operations, providing up-to-date information on project status, environmental conditions, or system performance.

Enhancing Mind Mapping with IoT Integration

1. **Dynamic Data Feeds:**
   - IoT devices, such as sensors and smart devices, can provide continuous data streams that update mind maps in real-time. This capability is invaluable for projects that require constant monitoring and quick responsiveness, such as in fields like logistics, manufacturing, and urban planning.
   - For example, a mind map used in a manufacturing setting could display real-time metrics on production levels, equipment status, and supply chain logistics, allowing managers to identify issues and make decisions promptly.

2. **Context-Aware Decision Making:**
   - By integrating data from IoT devices, AI-enhanced mind maps can become context-aware, adjusting displayed information based on the user's location, time, or specific conditions detected by IoT sensors.
   - In an environmental monitoring scenario, a mind map could dynamically adjust to show data relevant to a specific geographic area or environmental condition, aiding researchers or decision-makers in understanding local challenges and responses.

Technical Implementation and Challenges

1. **Interoperability and Standardization:**
   - Integrating IoT with mind mapping tools requires ensuring that devices from various manufacturers can communicate

effectively. This involves addressing issues of interoperability and data standardization, so that devices use a unified format that the mind mapping tool can process and visualize.

- Standardization bodies and industry consortia often play roles in establishing IoT protocols that facilitate this kind of interoperability.

2. **Security and Privacy Considerations:**

- The integration of IoT devices with mind mapping tools raises significant security and privacy concerns, as IoT devices are known for being vulnerable to hacking and data breaches. Ensuring robust security protocols and data encryption is crucial to protect sensitive information.

- Additionally, mind mapping tools must comply with privacy regulations, ensuring that data collected and displayed is done so with user consent and in compliance with laws such as GDPR.

Practical Applications and Benefits

1. **Enhanced Project Management:**

- In project management, IoT-enabled AI mind maps can offer project leaders real-time visibility into every aspect of the project. For instance, integrating IoT data can help track the progress of construction sites, the availability of resources, and the performance of deployed teams.

- This integration ensures that project managers have a holistic view of operations, helping them to anticipate delays and allocate resources more effectively.

2. **Smart City and Urban Planning:**

- For urban planners, IoT-integrated mind maps can collate data from various city systems, such as traffic lights, public transport vehicles, and energy systems, providing a comprehensive view of urban dynamics.

- This capability allows for better planning and quicker adjustments to urban infrastructure, enhancing city management and citizen services.

The fusion of IoT technology with AI in mind mapping tools is paving the way for more dynamic, informed, and responsive planning and decision-making across multiple industries. By leveraging real-time data from IoT devices, these tools can provide users with up-to-date insights, enhancing the effectiveness and efficiency of various projects and operations. As technology evolves, the integration of IoT with mind mapping will continue to break new ground, offering even more innovative ways to manage and visualize complex information systems.

Enhanced User Experience and Accessibility

Augmented Reality (AR) and Virtual Reality (VR):

AR and VR are set to transform mind mapping from a primarily visual experience into an immersive one. Users can engage with 3D mind maps in virtual spaces, manipulating information spatially and collaboratively with others in real-time, regardless of geographical limitations.

AR and VR in AI-Enhanced Mind Mapping

1. **Immersive Visualization:**
   - AR and VR technologies allow for the creation of immersive mind maps that users can navigate and interact with in a three-dimensional environment. This capability can be particularly beneficial for visualizing complex systems or networks, such as organizational charts, large-scale project plans, or even neural network structures.
   - By moving beyond flat, two-dimensional representations, AR and VR enable a more natural understanding of spatial

relationships and hierarchies within data, which can enhance cognitive processing and memory retention.

2. **Interactive Engagement:**
   - Beyond viewing, AR and VR enable users to interact directly with mind maps using gestures, voice commands, or controllers. This interaction can involve moving, linking, or editing nodes in real-time, individually or collaboratively with others, regardless of their physical location.
   - Such interactive capabilities make AR and VR ideal for collaborative sessions, workshops, or educational settings where participants can co-create and manipulate mind maps as if they were tangible objects in a shared space.

Technical Implementation and Integration Challenges

1. **Hardware and Accessibility:**
   - One of the primary barriers to widespread adoption of AR and VR in mind mapping is the requirement for specific hardware, such as VR headsets or AR-capable devices. These technologies, while increasingly affordable, are not yet ubiquitous.
   - To address accessibility concerns, developers are exploring less hardware-intensive AR applications that can run on smartphones and tablets, broadening the potential user base.

2. **Seamless Integration with AI:**
   - Integrating AR and VR with AI-driven mind mapping tools involves synchronizing the AI's analytical capabilities with the immersive interfaces provided by AR/VR. This requires robust backend architectures that can process AI analyses in real-time and render them effectively in a virtual space.

- Ensuring that the AI's insights and the user's interactions are seamlessly incorporated into the AR/VR environment poses significant technical challenges, particularly concerning real-time data processing and visualization fidelity.

Practical Applications and Broader Implications

1. **Enhanced Educational Tools:**
    - In educational contexts, AR and VR can revolutionize how students learn complex subjects. By engaging with interactive, three-dimensional mind maps, students can explore concepts like molecular biology, astronomy, or historical timelines in a manner that is both intuitive and memorable.
    - These technologies also offer unique opportunities for special education, where tailored, immersive experiences can cater to diverse learning needs and styles, making education more inclusive.
2. **Advanced Project and Data Management:**
    - In professional settings, AR and VR can facilitate more effective project management and data analysis. Teams can utilize spatial mind maps to manage large datasets or oversee project workflows, identifying connections and dependencies more clearly and making strategic decisions more confidently.
    - The ability to "walk through" a project's stages or a dataset's structure in virtual space can provide insights that might be missed on a traditional screen.

The integration of AR and VR with AI in mind mapping is poised to redefine the boundaries of how information is visualized and interacted with. These technologies not only promise to enhance the user experience by offering more immersive and intuitive ways to engage with data but also aim to make sophisticated mind mapping tools more accessible and beneficial across various fields and applications. As AR and VR continue to evolve, their convergence with AI-driven mind mapping will likely unlock unprecedented opportunities for innovation in visualization, collaboration, and decision-making.\

Adaptive Interfaces and Personalization:

Future mind mapping tools will increasingly leverage AI to offer adaptive user interfaces that adjust to individual user preferences and working styles. AI algorithms can learn from user interactions to personalize the tool's functionality, improving user experience and productivity.

Adaptive Interfaces in Mind Mapping

1. **User-Centric Design:**
   - Adaptive interfaces in mind mapping tools dynamically adjust the user interface based on the user's behavior, preferences, and context. This includes automatic adjustments of visual elements such as layout, color schemes, and information density based on the user's interaction patterns or specific tasks at hand.
   - For instance, if a user frequently zooms in on specific types of data or prefers certain types of visual representations (like graphs vs. lists), the mind mapping tool could automatically present information in the preferred formats, enhancing usability and satisfaction.

2. **Context-Aware Functionality:**
   - Beyond visual customization, adaptive interfaces can also adjust functionalities offered to the user based on the context of their work. If the system recognizes that the user is in a planning phase of a project, it might prioritize and suggest tools related to scheduling and resource allocation.

- Such context-awareness not only makes the tool more intuitive but also helps streamline the user's workflow, reducing cognitive load and boosting productivity.

Personalization Through AI

1. **Learning User Preferences:**
   - Machine learning algorithms are at the heart of personalization in AI-driven mind mapping tools. These algorithms analyze historical usage data to learn individual preferences and patterns, which inform how the mind mapping tool interacts with the user.
   - For example, if a user consistently organizes information in a certain hierarchical manner, the AI could suggest similar structures when the user starts a new mind map, speeding up the creation process and ensuring consistency.

2. **Predictive Assistance:**
   - AI can anticipate the user's needs based on past interactions and current activity within the mind map. This might include suggesting nodes that are likely to be added based on the existing content or alerting the user to potential connections that have not yet been explicitly drawn.
   - Predictive assistance can significantly enhance the depth and completeness of a mind map, especially in complex projects where oversight might lead to gaps in information.

Implementation Challenges and Considerations

1. **Balancing Automation and Control:**
   - One of the key challenges in implementing adaptive interfaces and personalization is ensuring that automation does not override user control. Users must be able to easily

override AI suggestions or revert to standard settings if they prefer, maintaining a balance between AI assistance and user autonomy.

2. **Privacy and Data Security:**

   ○ Personalization and adaptive features require collecting and analyzing user data, raising significant privacy and security concerns. Ensuring that data is handled securely and that users are informed about what data is collected and how it is used is crucial for maintaining trust.

   ○ Compliance with global data protection regulations, such as GDPR, is essential for any tool that incorporates personalization features based on user data.

The future of AI in mind mapping with adaptive interfaces and personalization holds immense potential to transform how users interact with mind mapping tools. By creating more intuitive and customized experiences, these technologies can make mind mapping more accessible and effective for a broader range of users across various disciplines. As these tools evolve, the emphasis will be on refining AI capabilities to better understand and adapt to user needs, ultimately making mind mapping an indispensable part of decision-making and creative processes.

Emerging trends and technologies are rapidly shaping the future integration of AI with mind mapping, making these tools more powerful, interactive, and indispensable across various fields. As these technologies continue to evolve, they promise to unlock new potentials for mind mapping, turning it into a versatile platform for visualization, analysis, and collaboration that is seamlessly integrated with the latest advancements in AI and computing.

Potential Developments in AI:

The future of Artificial Intelligence (AI) in mind mapping looks promising, with several emerging AI technologies poised to revolutionize how mind maps are created, utilized, and shared. As AI continues to evolve, its integration into mind mapping tools is expected to enhance their functionality, making them smarter, more interactive, and more adaptable to user needs.

Advanced Predictive Analytics and Decision Support

Scenario Modeling and Simulations:

Future AI developments could include sophisticated scenario modeling tools that allow users to simulate different decision pathways directly within mind maps. By using AI to predict outcomes based on varying inputs and conditions, users can visually explore potential consequences of different decisions, enhancing strategic planning and risk management.

Enhancing Strategic Decision-Making with Scenario Modeling

1. **Dynamic Scenario Generation:**
   - AI-driven mind mapping tools can use predictive analytics to automatically generate various future scenarios based on existing data and potential decisions. By manipulating different variables within the mind map, users can see how changes in one area might affect other parts of the system or the end goals.
   - This type of modeling is invaluable for strategic planning, allowing organizations to explore the potential impacts of their decisions before committing resources. For instance, a business could simulate market responses to a new product launch or changes in investment strategies.

2. **Risk Assessment and Contingency Planning:**
   - Integrating scenario simulations in mind maps helps organizations identify potential risks and develop contingency plans. AI can highlight possible risk factors and model their impacts under different conditions, providing a visual roadmap of potential challenges and their solutions.

- This proactive approach to risk management is critical in fields like finance, project management, and corporate strategy, where understanding and mitigating risks can mean the difference between success and failure.

Technical Implementation of Scenario Modeling in Mind Maps

1. **Integration with Data Analytics Platforms:**
   - For effective scenario modeling, AI-enhanced mind mapping tools need to be integrated with broader data analytics platforms. This integration allows for the seamless import and export of data, enabling the mind map to utilize comprehensive datasets for more accurate modeling.
   - This can involve real-time data feeds from internal databases or external sources, ensuring that the scenarios reflect the most current information available.
2. **Utilization of Machine Learning Algorithms:**
   - Machine learning algorithms are at the core of dynamic scenario modeling. These algorithms can analyze historical data to identify trends and patterns, which are used to predict how these patterns might evolve under different scenarios.
   - Continuous learning mechanisms allow these models to improve over time, adjusting their predictions based on new data and outcomes, thus enhancing the accuracy and relevance of the simulations.

Challenges and Considerations

1. **Complexity and Usability:**
   - Implementing sophisticated scenario modeling within mind maps can increase the complexity of the tool. Ensuring that these advanced features are user-friendly

and accessible to non-experts is crucial for widespread adoption.

- Developing intuitive interfaces and providing ample user support and training will be essential to help users navigate and make the most of these complex tools.

2. **Ethical and Bias Considerations:**

- As with all AI applications, there is a risk of inherent biases in the data or algorithms used for scenario modeling. It is crucial to continuously monitor and audit the models to ensure they do not perpetuate or amplify unwanted biases.
- Ensuring transparency in how scenarios are generated and providing users with the ability to adjust or question the underlying assumptions can help mitigate these risks.

The integration of scenario modeling and simulations into AI-enhanced mind mapping tools holds tremendous potential for transforming how decisions are made and risks are managed across various sectors. By enabling dynamic and predictive scenario planning directly within mind maps, organizations can gain a clearer, more actionable understanding of potential futures, making strategic decisions more informed and data-driven. As this technology advances, it will continue to expand the capabilities of mind mapping tools, making them indispensable instruments for strategic analysis and decision-making.

Real-Time Predictive Insights:

AI could be enhanced to provide real-time insights and recommendations while users are building mind maps. For example, AI could analyze the developing structure of a mind map and suggest areas that need more detailed exploration or point out imbalances in information distribution.

Enhancing Decision-Making with Real-Time Predictive Insights

1. **Proactive Information Delivery:**

- AI-driven mind mapping tools can analyze ongoing data inputs and user interactions to deliver real-time insights that anticipate the user's needs. For example, while a user is organizing data about market trends, the AI could predict and highlight emerging market opportunities or risks before the user explicitly identifies them.
- This proactive delivery of information helps users stay ahead of developments, enabling more timely and informed decisions.

2. **Contextual and Situational Awareness:**

- By integrating real-time data from various sources, AI-enhanced mind maps can provide contextual insights that are specific to the time and situation. For instance, if a user is working on a project mind map, the tool can integrate the latest project metrics to suggest adjustments or highlight potential bottlenecks.
- This level of situational awareness is particularly beneficial in fast-paced environments such as financial trading, emergency management, or dynamic project settings where conditions can change rapidly.

Technical Implementation of Real-Time Predictive Insights

1. **Integration with Live Data Streams:**

- To enable real-time predictive insights, mind mapping tools must be capable of integrating with live data streams from internal and external sources. This could include real-time market data, social media feeds, IoT device outputs, or live operational data from business processes.
- The challenge lies in efficiently processing and analyzing these vast streams of data in real-time to extract relevant insights without overwhelming the user.

2. **Advanced Analytics and Machine Learning Models:**

- Implementing real-time insights requires sophisticated machine learning models that can quickly analyze new data as it becomes available. These models must be trained to recognize patterns, predict outcomes, and learn continuously from new data to improve their accuracy and relevance.
- Leveraging technologies like stream processing and edge computing can help in handling the computational demands of real-time data analysis, ensuring that insights are delivered swiftly and reliably.

Challenges and Strategic Considerations

1. **Balancing Insight with Overload:**
   - One of the primary challenges in providing real-time predictive insights is to deliver valuable information without overwhelming the user with constant updates or irrelevant data. Mind mapping tools must be designed to filter and prioritize insights based on the user's current focus and preferences.
   - Customizable alert settings and insight filters can help users manage the flow of information, ensuring that they receive only the most pertinent insights.

2. **Accuracy and Trustworthiness:**
   - The effectiveness of real-time predictive insights heavily relies on the accuracy and trustworthiness of the AI models used. Inaccurate predictions can lead to misguided decisions, potentially having significant negative consequences.
   - Regular auditing, transparent methodologies, and user feedback loops are essential to maintain the integrity and reliability of predictive insights.

The potential of real-time predictive insights in AI-enhanced mind mapping is vast, offering users the ability to not only organize information but also to anticipate and react to future developments as they occur. As AI technology continues to advance, these capabilities will become more sophisticated, further empowering users to make proactive, data-informed decisions. This integration signifies a shift towards more dynamic, intelligent, and predictive mind mapping tools, poised to redefine strategic planning and decision support across multiple disciplines.

Enhanced Natural Language Processing

Semantic Understanding and Generation:

Future advancements in Natural Language Processing (NLP) could enable mind mapping tools to understand and generate content with a higher level of semantic awareness. AI would be able to summarize complex documents into mind maps, identify key themes and topics from large text volumes, and even suggest new areas of research based on the content.

Advancements in Semantic Understanding and Generation

1. **Deep Semantic Analysis:**
   - Future developments in NLP will likely include more sophisticated models for deep semantic analysis, enabling AI to understand context, subtleties, and complex meanings within text. This capability allows mind mapping tools to interpret user inputs more accurately and transform raw data (like academic articles, business reports, etc.) into structured, meaningful mind map nodes and connections.
   - For instance, when a user inputs a lengthy document into the mind map tool, AI could automatically distill the content into key themes and concepts, organizing them into a coherent structure that mirrors the document's inherent logic and informational hierarchy.

2. **Context-Aware Content Generation:**

- Enhanced NLP can enable mind mapping tools to generate content that is not only grammatically correct but also contextually appropriate. This involves creating summaries, annotations, or even new content suggestions that are aligned with the existing data within the mind map.
- For example, if a user is building a mind map about renewable energy, the AI could suggest adding nodes related to recent advancements or unresolved challenges in the field, pulling from the latest research or news sources.

Technical Implementation of Enhanced NLP

1. **Integration with Machine Learning and AI Models:**
   - Implementing advanced NLP in mind mapping tools requires the integration of state-of-the-art machine learning models, such as those based on transformer architectures like BERT or GPT, which are known for their effectiveness in language understanding and generation.
   - These models can be finc-tuned to specific domains or types of data to enhance their accuracy and relevance, providing tailored assistance based on the user's field of work or interest.
2. **Real-Time Language Processing:**
   - For NLP to be effective in mind mapping, it must operate in real time, quickly processing user inputs and integrating new data without delays. This necessitates powerful computational resources and optimized algorithms that can handle complex language tasks efficiently.
   - Additionally, maintaining a seamless user experience while performing these sophisticated language tasks in the background is crucial for the practical usability of AI-driven mind mapping tools.

Challenges and Future Directions

1. **Handling Linguistic Diversity:**
   - One of the challenges with semantic understanding and generation is dealing with the vast diversity of human language, including idioms, jargon, and dialects. Future developments in NLP must focus on increasing the linguistic versatility of AI to accommodate a wider range of languages and cultural contexts.
   - Multi-lingual and cross-lingual NLP capabilities will be essential for global applications of AI-enhanced mind mapping, ensuring that users worldwide can benefit from intelligent language processing.

2. **Ethical Considerations and Bias Mitigation:**
   - As with all AI technologies, there is a need to address ethical considerations and mitigate bias in language processing algorithms. Ensuring that NLP models are trained on diverse, unbiased datasets and regularly evaluated for fairness is critical.
   - Transparency in how language processing models work and allowing users to understand and if necessary, correct or override AI-generated content, are also important for maintaining trust and integrity in AI-enhanced mind mapping tools.

Enhanced NLP capabilities in semantic understanding and generation hold the potential to significantly transform AI-enhanced mind mapping tools, making them more intelligent, responsive, and useful across various disciplines. As NLP technology continues to evolve, it will enable mind mapping tools to become more than just visual aids, evolving into comprehensive, AI-driven platforms that can interpret, process, and generate knowledge dynamically, catering to the sophisticated needs of users in an information-driven world.

Voice-Driven Mind Mapping:

As voice recognition technology improves, AI could enable entirely voice-driven mind mapping, where users can create, modify, and navigate mind maps using spoken commands. This would make mind mapping more accessible, particularly for users with disabilities or those who prefer auditory learning and communication styles.

Voice-Driven Interactivity in Mind Mapping

1. **Hands-Free Operation:**
   - Voice-driven mind mapping allows users to create, edit, and navigate their mind maps without the need for physical interaction. This is particularly beneficial in scenarios where manual data entry is impractical or inconvenient, such as during brainstorming sessions, meetings, or while multitasking in dynamic work environments.
   - For instance, a project manager could verbally instruct the mind map to add tasks, assign roles, or update the status of different project components, all while discussing project details in a meeting without breaking the flow of conversation.

2. **Enhanced Accessibility:**
   - Voice commands open up mind mapping tools to a broader audience, including individuals with disabilities who may find traditional keyboard and mouse interfaces challenging. This accessibility can significantly democratize the use of mind mapping in education, business, and personal planning.
   - It also enhances the utility of mind mapping tools in educational settings, where students with different learning styles and abilities can engage with content more effectively through verbal interaction.

Technical Implementation of Voice-Driven Mind Mapping

1. **Integration with Advanced NLP Technologies:**
   - Implementing voice-driven capabilities requires the integration of sophisticated NLP technologies that can accurately recognize, interpret, and process spoken language. This involves not only recognizing words but also understanding context, intent, and nuance in the user's speech.
   - Technologies such as Google's BERT or OpenAI's GPT series provide models that can be fine-tuned for specific applications like mind mapping, enhancing the tool's ability to comprehend and respond to complex commands accurately.

2. **Real-Time Processing and Feedback:**
   - For voice-driven mind mapping to be effective, it must provide immediate processing of voice commands and instant feedback to the user. This real-time interaction helps maintain a smooth and efficient workflow, ensuring that the tool keeps pace with the user's thought processes and verbal instructions.
   - Achieving this level of responsiveness requires robust backend architectures that can handle rapid data processing and are optimized for low latency.

Challenges and Considerations

1. **Voice Recognition Accuracy:**
   - The accuracy of voice recognition, especially in noisy environments or with accents and dialects, remains a challenge. Continuous improvements in speech recognition algorithms and training with diverse speech data are essential to enhance accuracy.
   - Multi-microphone arrays and noise cancellation technologies can also be integrated to improve voice input clarity, making the system more reliable in varied settings.

2. **Privacy and Security Concerns:**
   - Voice data is inherently personal, and storing or processing this data raises significant privacy and security concerns. Implementing robust security measures, such as end-to-end encryption and secure voice data storage, is critical to protect user privacy.
   - Additionally, ensuring compliance with global privacy regulations (like GDPR) when handling voice data is crucial for maintaining user trust and legal compliance.

Voice-driven mind mapping powered by AI and enhanced NLP is poised to significantly alter how users interact with mind mapping tools, offering a more natural, efficient, and accessible way to organize thoughts and manage information. As this technology evolves, it holds the promise to make mind mapping an integral part of more interactive and productive workspaces, tailored to meet the diverse needs and preferences of users across various domains.

Machine Vision Integration

Image and Video Integration:

With advances in machine vision, AI-enhanced mind mapping tools could incorporate image and video content more effectively. AI could analyze visual media to extract relevant information and automatically generate or update mind maps based on this analysis.

Enhancing Mind Maps with Image and Video Integration

1. **Automated Content Extraction:**
   - Machine vision can automate the extraction of relevant information from images and videos directly into mind maps. For instance, AI could analyze a video from a conference and automatically create mind map nodes that summarize key points, detect speaker identities, and link to specific timestamps in the video for quick reference.

- Similarly, images such as infographics or charts can be scanned by AI to extract and organize data into a mind map, making complex information easily accessible and understandable.

2. Enhanced Multimedia Nodes:

- Mind maps can be enriched with multimedia nodes that not only link to external image or video resources but also display embedded previews directly within the map. Machine vision can help in dynamically selecting and displaying the most relevant parts of a video or segments of an image within these nodes.
- This capability significantly enhances the utility of mind maps in fields like education, marketing, and research, where visual aids are crucial for explaining and retaining complex information.

Technical Implementation of Image and Video Integration

1. Real-Time Image and Video Processing:

- Implementing machine vision in mind mapping tools requires the capability to process image and video data in real time. This involves using algorithms for object recognition, pattern detection, and semantic analysis to understand and categorize visual content accurately.
- Advanced processing techniques, such as convolutional neural networks (CNNs) and other deep learning models, are typically employed to handle these tasks, offering both speed and accuracy in visual data analysis.

2. Integration with Existing Data Architectures:

- For effective image and video integration, mind mapping tools need to be seamlessly integrated with existing data architectures that handle multimedia storage, retrieval, and streaming. This integration ensures that visual data is readily available for inclusion in mind maps and can be efficiently managed within the broader data ecosystem of the organization.

- Ensuring scalability and performance optimization in handling large volumes of multimedia data is critical to maintain system responsiveness and user satisfaction.

Challenges and Strategic Considerations

1. **Data Volume and Management:**
   - The inclusion of high volumes of image and video data in mind maps can lead to significant increases in data storage requirements and management complexity. Efficient data compression techniques, cloud storage solutions, and content delivery networks (CDNs) may be necessary to manage this challenge effectively.
   - Organizing and indexing large multimedia libraries for quick access and integration into mind maps also requires sophisticated database management and search algorithms.
2. **Quality and Relevance of Visual Content:**
   - Ensuring the quality and relevance of automatically extracted visual content is a significant challenge. Machine vision systems must be finely tuned to discriminate between pertinent and non-pertinent visual information to avoid cluttering the mind map with irrelevant data.
   - Continuous learning and adaptation, where the system refines its selection criteria based on user feedback and interaction patterns, can help improve the relevance and quality of integrated content over time.

The integration of machine vision technologies with AI-enhanced mind mapping tools opens up new possibilities for incorporating rich visual data into mind maps, enhancing their effectiveness as tools for information visualization and analysis. As machine vision technology continues to advance, it will enable more sophisticated and seamless integration of images and videos, transforming mind maps into dynamic, multimedia-enhanced decision-making and learning aids.

Collaborative and Augmented Reality Features

Enhanced Collaborative Tools:

Future AI developments could focus on improving collaborative features in mind mapping tools, allowing for more dynamic interaction among users in real-time. AI could manage the contributions of different users, ensuring that the mind map remains organized and coherent even with multiple contributors.

Advancements in AI-Driven Collaborative Mind Mapping

1. **Real-Time Synchronization and Interaction:**
   - AI can significantly enhance the capabilities of mind mapping tools to support real-time collaboration. Through AI algorithms, these tools can synchronize changes made by multiple users instantly, ensuring all participants have up-to-date information. This synchronization includes not only text but also multimedia elements, annotations, and even structural changes to the mind maps.
   - Real-time AI analytics can also provide instant insights based on the collective input, offering suggestions, highlighting discrepancies, or identifying emerging patterns that might not be obvious to individual participants.

2. **Context-Aware Collaboration:**
   - In collaborative sessions, AI can enhance the user experience by adapting the mind map based on the context of the meeting and the roles of participants. For instance, AI could highlight information relevant to specific users or control access to certain parts of the mind map based on user permissions and the focus of the discussion.

- Context-aware tools can automatically adjust the display and complexity of information to fit the needs of different groups, such as technical vs. non-technical stakeholders, thereby streamlining communication and enhancing productivity.

Integration of Augmented Reality in Collaborative Mind Mapping

1. **Immersive AR Workspaces:**
   - Augmented Reality can transform traditional mind mapping by creating an immersive workspace where participants can interact with a virtual mind map as if it were a physical object in their environment. This approach allows users to use natural gestures to manipulate elements of the map, such as dragging nodes, drawing connections, or zooming in on specific details.
   - AR-enhanced mind maps can be particularly effective in brainstorming sessions or strategic planning meetings, where the spatial arrangement of information and the ability to physically interact with data can lead to deeper engagement and understanding.
2. **Enhanced Remote Collaboration:**
   - With AR, remote participants can feel as though they are present in the same room, interacting with the same physical objects. This presence can dramatically improve the effectiveness of remote meetings, making them more engaging than traditional video calls or shared screens.
   - AR can also overlay additional information onto the users' real-world view, such as live data feeds, performance metrics, or even facial expressions and body language cues of other participants, enhancing communication and emotional connection among team members.

Challenges and Future Directions

1. Technology Integration and Accessibility:

- ○ Integrating AR and advanced collaborative features into mind mapping tools requires seamless technology integration that may involve significant hardware and software investments. Ensuring these tools are accessible and affordable for a wide range of users remains a challenge.
- ○ Developing lightweight, web-based AR applications or supporting lower-cost AR devices can help mitigate these barriers, making advanced collaborative mind mapping more widely accessible.

2. User Training and Adaptation:

- ○ The successful adoption of these advanced tools requires effective user training and support. Participants need to feel comfortable with the new technologies to fully leverage their capabilities.
- ○ Ongoing user education, intuitive design, and responsive technical support are crucial to facilitate the adoption and effective use of these innovative collaborative tools.

The potential for AI to enhance collaborative mind mapping tools, particularly through the integration of augmented reality features, represents a significant advancement in how collaborative and creative processes are facilitated. These technologies promise not only to enhance the functionality and interactivity of mind mapping tools but also to redefine the paradigms of teamwork and collective problem-solving across industries. As these technologies continue to develop, they will undoubtedly unlock new and exciting possibilities for enhancing collaboration and driving innovation.

Ethical AI Development and Implementation

Bias Mitigation and Ethical Guidelines:

As AI becomes more central to mind mapping, developing ethical AI algorithms that minimize bias and ensure fairness will be crucial. Future developments should focus on creating transparent AI systems where users can understand and trust how the AI operates and makes decisions.

Importance of Bias Mitigation in AI-Enhanced Mind Mapping

1. **Understanding and Identifying Biases:**
   - AI systems, including those used in mind mapping, can inadvertently learn and perpetuate biases present in their training data. These biases could skew the AI's functionality, leading to unfair or unethical outcomes. For instance, an AI that suggests content based on user interactions might favor certain viewpoints or exclude minority perspectives if not properly checked.
   - It's crucial for developers to implement procedures to identify and understand the sources of bias, which could include historical data trends, user feedback loops, or inherent biases in data collection processes.

2. **Implementing Bias Mitigation Techniques:**
   - Techniques such as diverse data sampling, employing fairness algorithms, and continuous monitoring of outcomes are essential to mitigate bias. These methods help ensure that AI models provide balanced insights and do not discriminate against any group or individual.
   - Regular audits by independent third parties can also help identify and correct biases that internal checks might miss, ensuring the AI remains fair and objective over time.

Establishing Ethical Guidelines for AI in Mind Mapping

1. **Development of Ethical Standards:**

- Establishing clear ethical guidelines is critical for AI development, especially in tools used for decision-making and strategic planning like mind mapping. These guidelines should cover aspects such as transparency, user privacy, data security, and the inclusivity of different user groups.
- Ethical standards should be developed in consultation with ethicists, technologists, and end-users to cover all possible ethical concerns comprehensively and practically.

2. **Ensuring Transparency and Accountability:**
   - Transparency in AI involves clear communication about how the AI operates, how data is used, and how decisions are made. For mind mapping tools, this means users should understand how the AI generates suggestions, integrates data, and can potentially influence decisions.
   - Accountability mechanisms should be in place to address any issues that arise from AI operations. This includes establishing clear lines of responsibility and having procedures to handle complaints or concerns about the AI's decisions or behavior.

Challenges and Future Directions

1. **Balancing Innovation with Ethical Considerations:**
   - One of the key challenges in ethical AI development is balancing the push for innovative, cutting-edge technologies with the need to ensure these technologies are developed responsibly. Innovators must consider the ethical implications of their designs from the outset, integrating ethics into the development process rather than as an afterthought.
   - Engaging with stakeholders from diverse backgrounds can help achieve this balance, ensuring that various

perspectives are considered in shaping the ethical landscape of AI-enhanced mind mapping.

2. **Adapting to Evolving Ethical Standards:**
   - Ethical standards for AI are continuously evolving as our understanding of AI's impact deepens and as societal values change. Mind mapping tools that utilize AI must be adaptable, with mechanisms to update ethical guidelines and implementation strategies as new ethical challenges emerge.
   - Ongoing education and training for developers and users about ethical AI use are crucial to keep up with these changes and ensure that mind mapping tools remain tools for positive transformation.

The ethical development and implementation of AI in mind mapping are crucial not only to prevent harm but also to maximize the technology's benefits. By focusing on bias mitigation and establishing robust ethical guidelines, developers can ensure that AI-enhanced mind mapping tools are fair, transparent, and accountable. This responsible approach fosters trust among users and helps realize the full potential of AI in enhancing strategic and creative processes through mind mapping.

The potential developments in AI promise to further revolutionize mind mapping, making it an even more powerful tool for visualization, analysis, and collaboration. As these technologies advance, they will open new possibilities for enhancing how individuals and organizations conceptualize, plan, and execute their ideas. The key to harnessing these advancements will lie in thoughtful integration, user-centered design, and ethical AI practices, ensuring that mind mapping tools continue to evolve as valuable assets in the digital age.

Challenges and Opportunities:

The integration of Artificial Intelligence (AI) into mind mapping presents a range of challenges and opportunities that could significantly influence its adoption and effectiveness. As organizations and individuals consider integrating AI-enhanced tools into their strategic and creative processes, understanding these factors is crucial for successful implementation.

Challenges in Adopting AI-Enhanced Mind Mapping

Technical Complexity and Integration:

Challenge: Implementing AI within mind mapping tools involves complex technical integration with existing IT systems and data infrastructures. Organizations may face challenges related to compatibility, data migration, and maintaining system performance.

Mitigation: Careful planning and phased implementation can help manage these technical challenges. Additionally, choosing AI solutions that offer flexible integration options and robust support can ease the transition.

User Adoption and Change Management:

Challenge: Resistance to change is a common hurdle in adopting new technologies. Users accustomed to traditional mind mapping methods may be hesitant to adopt new AI-enhanced tools, especially if they perceive them as overly complex or intrusive.

Mitigation: Effective change management strategies, including comprehensive training programs, user engagement initiatives, and clear communication about the benefits of AI-enhanced tools, are essential. Demonstrating tangible improvements in productivity or decision-making can also help win over skeptics.

Data Privacy and Security:

Challenge: AI-enhanced mind mapping tools often require access to sensitive or proprietary information. Ensuring the privacy and security of this data is a major concern, especially under stringent data protection regulations like GDPR.

Mitigation: Implementing advanced cybersecurity measures and ensuring compliance with data protection laws are critical. Transparency about data usage policies and providing users control over their data can further enhance trust and security.

Opportunities in Adopting AI-Enhanced Mind Mapping

Enhanced Decision-Making and Insights:

Opportunity: AI can process vast amounts of data to provide insights and predictions that are not easily achievable through manual methods. This capability can transform mind maps from static visual tools into dynamic decision-support systems that offer real-time insights and forecasts.

Impact: Organizations can leverage these enhanced capabilities to improve strategic planning, project management, and innovation processes, leading to better outcomes and competitive advantages.

Improved Collaboration and Accessibility:

Opportunity: AI-enhanced mind mapping tools can facilitate better collaboration across teams, including remote and distributed workforces. Features like real-time updates, predictive analytics, and natural language processing can make collaboration more efficient and inclusive.

Impact: Enhanced collaboration can lead to more diverse input and quicker consensus, improving the quality and creativity of outcomes. Additionally, accessibility features powered by AI can make mind mapping tools more usable for individuals with disabilities, broadening the user base.

Scalability and Adaptability:

Opportunity: AI technologies are inherently scalable, allowing mind mapping tools to handle larger datasets and more complex information structures. AI can also adapt to the specific needs and preferences of users over time, personalizing the experience.

Impact: Scalable and adaptable tools can grow with the organization, ensuring that investments in AI-enhanced mind mapping remain relevant and valuable over time. Personalization can also increase user satisfaction and productivity.

The adoption of AI-enhanced mind mapping presents both significant challenges and substantial opportunities. While technical and organizational hurdles must be carefully managed, the potential benefits in terms of enhanced insights, improved collaboration, and greater scalability offer compelling reasons for integration. Organizations that effectively navigate these challenges and leverage the opportunities are likely to see considerable gains in their ability to organize, plan, and innovate.

Conclusion

The future of AI in mind mapping is rich with possibilities, driven by advancements in AI technology and its integration with other cutting-edge fields. These developments promise to make mind mapping more intuitive, powerful, and tailored to individual needs, transforming it into an indispensable tool for a wide range of applications. As this technology evolves, it will continue to open new horizons for creativity, planning, and strategic decision-making across all sectors.

12

Appendices

Glossary Of Terms:

An essential component of any comprehensive book on mind mapping, particularly those that delve into the technical and innovative aspects of using AI in mind mapping, is the inclusion of a glossary of terms. The glossary serves as a valuable resource for readers, ensuring that all readers, regardless of their prior knowledge or expertise, have a clear understanding of the terminology used throughout the book. This section will outline the importance, structure, and key considerations for compiling a glossary in the context of a book on AI-enhanced mind mapping.

Importance of a Glossary

1. **Clarification of Terms:**
   - The field of AI and mind mapping is replete with specialized terminology and jargon that can be complex and unfamiliar to many readers. A glossary provides clear and concise definitions, helping readers understand specific terms that are crucial to comprehending the content of the book.

2. **Enhancing Reader Engagement:**

- By demystifying terms and phrases, a glossary makes the material more accessible and engaging for a broader audience. This inclusivity is essential for educational texts, as it ensures that no reader is left behind due to a lack of understanding of the terminology.

3. **Reference Tool:**

- A glossary acts as a quick-reference tool that readers can use throughout their reading journey. This feature is particularly useful in academic or professional contexts where readers might need to recall the definition of a term quickly without disrupting their engagement with the material.

Structure of a Glossary

1. **Alphabetical Arrangement:**

- Terms in the glossary should be arranged alphabetically to facilitate easy navigation. Each term is followed by its definition, and possibly a brief example or annotation to illustrate its application, especially when the term pertains to processes or concepts in AI and mind mapping.

2. **Comprehensive Definitions:**

- Definitions should be precise yet comprehensive enough to provide a clear understanding without requiring readers to seek additional sources. Technical terms should be explained in layman's terms, but without oversimplifying complex concepts.

3. **Cross-Referencing:**

- Where relevant, the glossary can include cross-references to other terms within the glossary or to sections of the book where the term is discussed in detail. This helps to integrate the glossary more fully with the rest of the book and encourages a deeper exploration of the topics.

Key Considerations for a Mind Mapping Glossary

1. **Selection of Terms:**
   - Choosing which terms to include in the glossary involves consideration of the book's scope and the assumed knowledge level of the target audience. It is important to include all terms that are technical, newly introduced, or used in a specific context within the field of AI and mind mapping.
2. **Regular Updates:**
   - In fields as rapidly evolving as AI and mind mapping, new terms and usage can emerge frequently. Periodic updates to the glossary may be necessary to keep it relevant and useful, particularly in subsequent editions of the book or related publications.
3. **Accessibility:**
   - The glossary should be designed to be as accessible as possible, which might include the incorporation of visual aids for complex terms or concepts, or digital versions that include hyperlinks to additional resources or multimedia content for further explanation.

The inclusion of a well-organized and thoughtfully prepared glossary is a critical component of any book on AI-enhanced mind mapping. It not only aids in understanding and retention but also enhances the usability of the book as a reference tool. Careful attention to the clarity, accuracy, and accessibility of the glossary will significantly contribute to the overall effectiveness and reader satisfaction of the publication.

Directory Of AI Mind Mapping:

In a comprehensive book about AI-enhanced mind mapping, an appendix dedicated to a directory of AI mind mapping tools and resources is invaluable. This directory serves as a practical guide for readers, providing them with essential information about the tools and resources available in the field. It can help readers navigate the vast landscape of technologies, software, and educational materials, facilitating a deeper engagement with the book's content and further exploration of the subject matter. Here's how such a directory can be structured and its significance in enhancing the utility of the book.

Importance of a Directory of AI Mind Mapping Tools and Resources

1. **Practical Application:**
   - The directory connects theory with practice, allowing readers to see how the concepts discussed in the book can be applied using current technologies. This bridge between knowledge and application is crucial for learners and professionals alike to integrate new skills into their work or studies.

2. **Resource Accessibility:**
   - By compiling a list of tools and resources, the directory makes it easier for readers to access and utilize these technologies. It saves readers time and effort in searching for reputable sources and tools, providing a vetted starting point for exploration.

3. **Encouragement of Continued Learning:**
   - A well-curated directory encourages readers to continue their learning journey beyond the book. It provides pathways for further study and experimentation, which is particularly important in a rapidly evolving field like AI.

Structure of the Directory

1. **Categorization of Tools and Resources:**
   - The directory should be organized into categories based on tool types, usability, features, or target user groups.

Common categories might include free vs. paid tools, tools for educational purposes, professional-grade tools, and resources for developers looking to build custom solutions.

- ○ Each category can be introduced with a short description to help readers understand the distinctions and choose which category to explore based on their needs.

2. **Detailed Descriptions:**

- ○ For each tool or resource listed, provide a detailed description that includes its primary functions, unique features, possible use cases, and any specific requirements or compatibility issues. This information helps readers make informed decisions about which tools might be right for their specific applications.

3. **Links and Contact Information:**

- ○ Include hyperlinks to the tools' websites, and where applicable, contact information for the developers or vendors. This not only facilitates easy access but also allows readers to obtain support and more detailed information directly from the source.

Key Considerations for a Mind Mapping Tools Directory

1. **Accuracy and Currency:**

- ○ The technology landscape can change rapidly, with new tools emerging and existing ones being updated or phased out. It's important to ensure that the information in the directory is current and accurate at the time of publication, and to provide guidance on how readers can check for the most recent updates.

2. **Neutrality and Objectivity:**

- ○ The directory should aim to be neutral and objective, providing information without apparent bias towards any specific tool or resource. Recommendations should be based on functionality and user feedback rather than promotional interests.

3. **Legal and Ethical Considerations:**

   ○ Ensure that all recommendations comply with legal and ethical standards, particularly in terms of data privacy and security. It's also wise to include a disclaimer about the potential risks associated with downloading and using software, particularly from less well-known sources.

An appendix containing a directory of AI mind mapping tools and resources significantly enhances a book's practical value. It not only serves as a guide to the tools available but also encourages readers to actively engage with the technology, apply what they have learned, and continue exploring the field independently. This directory should be thoughtfully organized, regularly updated, and curated with the user's best interests in mind to be a valuable addition to the book.

Recommended Reading and References:

An essential component of any educational or informational book, particularly those on topics like AI-enhanced mind mapping, is the appendices section dedicated to recommended reading and references. This part of the book serves not only as a bibliographic resource but also as a guide to further exploration and deeper understanding of the subject matter. This section will discuss the structure, importance, and considerations for compiling a comprehensive list of recommended reading and references in the context of AI and mind mapping.

Importance of Recommended Reading and References

1. **Deepening Knowledge:**

   ○ A curated list of recommended readings allows readers to deepen their understanding of concepts discussed in the book. By directing readers to additional sources, authors can enhance their audience's learning experience and provide avenues for advanced study.

2. **Credibility and Scholarship:**
   - Including a thorough list of references underscores the scholarly rigor of the book. It shows the research undertaken during the writing process and provides a foundation upon which the book's assertions are based, thus enhancing its credibility.

3. **Resource for Continued Education:**
   - For students, professionals, and academics, the recommended reading and references section is a valuable resource for continued education and research. It can guide readers to seminal works, key debates, and cutting-edge research in the field.

Structure of Recommended Reading and References

1. **Thematic Organization:**
   - Organize the reading list and references thematically or by chapter to help readers easily find materials that expand on specific topics covered in the book. Each section can begin with a brief introduction explaining why these readings are essential and how they relate to the topics discussed.

2. **Annotation:**
   - Where possible, include annotations for each recommended reading. An annotation might summarize the content, explain its relevance, and suggest how the reader might use it to complement the material covered in the book. This not only adds value but also makes the list more user-friendly.

3. **Accessibility Information:**
   - Provide information on how to access the materials. For books and articles, include standard bibliographic

information. For online resources, provide URLs or DOIs. If some resources are behind paywalls or part of institutional subscriptions, indicate this and suggest possible open-access alternatives.

Key Considerations for a Mind Mapping Tools Directory

1. **Up-to-Date Resources:**
   - Ensure that the recommended readings and references are up to date, especially in fields like AI that evolve rapidly. Include the latest editions of books and recent articles where possible, and consider the publication date when recommending resources to ensure the information is not outdated.

2. **Diversity of Perspectives:**
   - Include a diverse range of voices and perspectives in the recommended readings to provide a well-rounded understanding of the topics. This can include foundational texts as well as critical or contemporary perspectives that challenge conventional wisdom.

3. **Practical and Theoretical Balances:**
   - Balance the recommendations between practical guides and theoretical texts. While practical guides help in applying concepts, theoretical texts will provide deeper insights and broader context, enriching the reader's understanding of AI and mind mapping.

Conclusion

The appendices section containing recommended reading and references is crucial for any book dealing with complex and rapidly evolving fields like AI-enhanced mind mapping. Not only does it enhance the reader's learning experience, but it also supports the book's academic integrity and aids in the professional development of its audience.

Thoughtfully compiled and organized, this section can significantly extend the impact and usefulness of the book, turning it into a launching pad for further exploration and discovery in the field.